# BIG GAY ADVENTURES IN EDUCATION

*Big Gay Adventures in Education* is a collection of true stories by 'out' teachers, and students of 'out' teachers, all about their experiences in schools. The book aims to empower LGBT+ teachers to be the role models they needed when they were in school and help all teachers and school leaders to promote LGBT+ visibility and inclusion.

The contributors range from trainee teachers to experienced school leaders and leading figures from the community across the LGBT+ spectrum, as well as LGBT+ students whose lives were improved by having an openly LGBT+ teacher. Each story is accompanied by an editor's note reflecting on the contributor's experience and the practical implications for schools and teachers in supporting LGBT+ young people and ensuring they feel safe and included in their school communities.

Compiled by the co-founder and director of LGBTed, the inspiring stories in this book are essential reading for LGBT+ teachers and allies. Let's be the role models we needed when we were at school and show our students that they can be successful and happy as an LGBT+ person.

**Daniel Tomlinson-Gray** is a secondary school Media Studies and English teacher with more than 12 years of experience who has also worked in school leadership. He is the co-founder and director of LGBTed with Hannah Jepson, working with teachers and schools to increase the visibility of authentic LGBT+ role models. He is married to Samuel, with a tabby cat called Missy Misdemeanour and two hens, Edina and Patsy.

# BIG GAY ADVENTURES IN EDUCATION

Supporting LGBT+ Visibility and Inclusion in Schools

Edited by Daniel Tomlinson-Gray

LONDON AND NEW YORK

First published 2021
by Routledge
2 Park Square, Milton Park, Abingdon, Oxon OX14 4RN

and by Routledge
52 Vanderbilt Avenue, New York, NY 10017

*Routledge is an imprint of the Taylor & Francis Group, an informa business*

© 2021 selection and editorial matter, Daniel Tomlinson-Gray; individual chapters, the contributors

The right of Daniel Tomlinson-Gray to be identified as the author of the editorial material, and of the authors for their individual chapters, has been asserted in accordance with sections 77 and 78 of the Copyright, Designs and Patents Act 1988.

All rights reserved. No part of this book may be reprinted or reproduced or utilised in any form or by any electronic, mechanical, or other means, now known or hereafter invented, including photocopying and recording, or in any information storage or retrieval system, without permission in writing from the publishers.

*Trademark notice*: Product or corporate names may be trademarks or registered trademarks, and are used only for identification and explanation without intent to infringe.

*British Library Cataloguing-in-Publication Data*
A catalogue record for this book is available from the British Library

*Library of Congress Cataloging-in-Publication Data*
A catalog record has been requested for this book

ISBN: 978-0-367-89421-4 (hbk)
ISBN: 978-0-367-89422-1 (pbk)
ISBN: 978-1-003-01908-4 (ebk)

Typeset in Palatino
by codeMantra

# CONTENTS

*Foreword*   vii
Andrew Moffatt MBE

1 **Why this book exists**   1
   *Daniel Tomlinson-Gray*

2 **To be out or not to be out**   7
   *Sue Sanders*

3 **It's OK: a school assembly**   13
   *David Lowbridge-Ellis*

4 **Miss, are you a lesbian? Becoming bisexual**   17
   *Adele Bates*

5 **Out from the outset**   23
   *Kip Webb-Heller*

6 **Permission**   29
   *Chris Mattley*

7 **A story in two halves**   35
   *Catherine Halliwell and Cerian Craske*

8 **Intersections of identity: being an 'out' Jewish bisexual teacher**   39
   *Allison Zionts*

9 **You can't win on culture alone, but you sure can lose on it**   43
   *James Bennett*

10 **Bi, Bi, Bi**   47
   *Molly Luscombe*

| | | |
|---|---|---|
| 11 | *That* assembly<br>Becca Adson | 51 |
| 12 | Simple acts of kindness and love<br>Callum Richardson | 55 |
| 13 | Add a little bit of glitter<br>Faye Cutting | 59 |
| 14 | 'Miss, I'm part of LGBT too'<br>Amy Ridler | 63 |
| 15 | The cupboard without a rainbow flag<br>Hadley Stewart | 67 |
| 16 | I want the world to know<br>Alison Riley | 71 |
| 17 | The best you can be is yourself<br>Zoe Defoe | 73 |
| 18 | You've gotta give 'em hope<br>Michael Williams | 81 |
| 19 | The invisible girl<br>Jennifer Heaton | 85 |
| 20 | The moderately successful lesbian<br>Nicola Sharp | 89 |
| 21 | The rainbow armadillo<br>Darrell Chart-Boyles | 95 |
| 22 | Being the role model I wish I had<br>Pam Stallard | 99 |
| 23 | Changing the narrative: why being 'out' at school is so important<br>Will Goldsmith | 105 |
| 24 | Being your authentic self at work<br>Hannah Jepson | 109 |

# FOREWORD
*Andrew Moffat MBE*

This book will make a valuable contribution to resources for those who want to explore equality in our schools and be reassured they are not alone on that journey. Statistics showing the level of homophobia that exists today in schools are well publicised and demonstrate the need for this book, but it is not only LGBT+ young people who struggle in classrooms; there are lost voices of lesbian, gay, bisexual, trans and others (LGBT+) teachers and staff, many hiding their identity as they do their jobs every day. This book will provide much needed support for those people but also for staff who do not identify as LGBT+, who are looking to develop inclusive practice in their workplace.

I hope the book will also provide reassurance to young people in school, as they realise LGBT+ people are all around us; yes, some of us teachers are also LGBT+ too! I want young people to question homophobia in their schools and think about the role they can take to reduce it. And there is another world outside education, where inclusive practice needs to be developed. Mental health and well-being are priorities in every workplace today, and this means creating an ethos where everyone feels comfortable about being who they are.

The real strength of this book is that it gives a voice to real stories by real people. In years to come we will look back on this time and be shocked at the level of homophobia that was allowed to exist in schools in 2020. It is my hope that this book will contribute to a reduction in the taboo and stigma that currently exists around teachers coming out in schools; we should be 'out' wherever we are, wherever we work, as we are in every other part of our lives.

I am full of confidence and hope for the future of inclusive practice in schools, and I am proud to be asked to write the foreword for this book, which I am sure will provide much needed support to teachers who want to make a difference.

With thanks,
Andrew Moffat, MBE
www.no-outsiders.com

# 1 Why this book exists
*Daniel Tomlinson-Gray*

*Daniel Tomlinson-Gray is a secondary school Media Studies and English teacher with more than 12 years of experience who has also worked in school leadership. He is now the co-founder and director of LGBTed with Hannah Jepson, working with teachers and school leaders to increase the visibility of authentic LGBT+ role models in schools. He is married to Samuel, has a cat called Missy Misdemeanour and two bantam hens called Edina & Patsy. Follow @LGBTedUK on Twitter.*

I did it. After nine years of teaching, I finally came out to my students. It shouldn't be such a big deal in this day and age, but sadly it is.

When I was at secondary school in 1990s Basingstoke, I had a horrendous time. I was subjected to bullying of the most horrific kind from Neanderthal knuckle-scraping "lads" almost daily. I was tormented for being gay for many years before I even knew that I was – they all seemed to know something I didn't and delighted in making my life hell. I had wet toilet roll thrown at me in the changing rooms; I had sandwiches thrown at me from the window of the school bus that I was too terrified to board; I was pushed around, kicked and punched in corridors; I was called names I didn't even understand, but I was never without a sassy comeback. My coping mechanism was to fight back with my vocabulary, to be the cleverest and strongest person I could be, to prove them all wrong. I disrupted the status quo, I was unapologetic and I owned it. Between the private tears and the personal agony, I owned it.

When I raised it with my teachers, in utter desperation, I was told "it's just something you have to deal with". This was during the time of Section 28, the vile anti-LGBT+ legislation that still leaves a scar in our schools to this day. My school didn't know how – and in fact wasn't permitted – to deal with it. These days, with hindsight, I say I was never a victim of homophobic bullying. I was subjected to it on a daily basis, but I was never a victim. I have fortunately had the strength of character to overcome it and use it to my advantage, but without positive role models, so many other vulnerable children are less fortunate. All young people should feel safe at school, be encouraged to thrive and be themselves. I wasn't.

I decided to become a teacher to give young people the opportunities I didn't have to make them feel safe and respected. It took a long time, however, to be fully honest about who I am for many reasons. When training to be a teacher more than 12 years ago, in a Catholic school, I was told emphatically that I should not tell students I'm gay. It would give them "more ammunition", I was told. In hindsight, isn't this kind of comment doing our young people a deep disservice? I think we grossly underestimate them when we assume their reaction won't be positive. It has taken me many years of working with our wonderful young people to know that comments like this do not reflect them. In my experience, they are more open-minded and accepting then many of their parents and many of my former colleagues. Comments like this force teachers and school leaders to stay "in the closet" and therefore to let down some of our most vulnerable students by not being a visible role model with whom they can identify. I believe lesbian, gay, bisexual, trans and others (LGBT+) teachers should lead by example where possible and that's why, as part of LGBT History Month in February 2017, I finally came out to over 1,000 students in assembly.

With a new headteacher at the school, I decided to broach the idea of commemorating LGBT History Month, and he was instantly supportive. I wanted to increase visibility of LGBT+ people and issues in our school and usualise it. I had arranged it so that all subjects were teaching about LGBT+ issues to all students for one lesson this month. In Geography, students were being taught about LGBT+ safe spaces and why some cities have a higher LGBT+ population. In Languages, they were being taught about Polari and in Maths they were learning about Alan Turing and his struggles, leading to his eventual suicide. As part of this range of events, I thought it would be a good idea to "come out" to the students in an assembly. Coming out is something I have instinctively wanted to do for some time – the final frontier, perhaps, in building an open and positive relationship with my students in school. If we're going to increase visibility and acceptance of the LGBT+ community, then we should start with ourselves as role models, yes? I thought about how it would have helped me to have an LGBT+ figure to look up to as a child and decided to go for it. What was the worst that could happen?

So I did it. No jazz hands, no drama, no hysteria. A couple of mouths fell open, there were a few gasps and awkward looks skyward, but the response amongst the students was mostly muted. Perhaps how it should be. I simply talked all about what, as a school, we were going to commemorate LGBT History Month and said, "as a gay man, I know how important it is to have positive role models." That was it. A few minutes after the assembly, one student – who I have never taught – came up to me and said "Sir, your assembly just literally changed my life" and awkwardly walked away, not wishing to cause a scene or, perhaps, "out" himself. I remember thinking that's why I did it, right there. I know now that I've probably made a difference to at least one life forever more and I can't put a price on that. No amount of backlash – which so far has been minimal – can take that way.

It's very telling that this was a much bigger deal than I ever imagined. It gained worldwide news coverage, particularly on the BBC, and the response to it has been phenomenal. I have received over 800 emails and messages of support from all over the world and also from former pupils. One man actually went to the trouble to hand-write a postcard, track down my work address and post it all the way to the UK from Texas, purely to thank me and say how "moved to tears" he was. I have since decided to use my profile to make a difference for all the young people who are like I was. It took me nine years to find the courage myself; therefore, I understand why most LGBT+ teachers don't come out. Coming out is of course deeply personal for everyone and has to be done on one's own terms. But I would encourage us all to do it for the sake of all those young people that need us. Maybe then it'll stop being a "big deal" and being "brave", and it will no longer make the news. It'll finally just be embraced as part of life.

## Why LGBTed

To help enable this, LGBTed was launched in 2018. It was a result of many months of ground work by Hannah Jepson and myself, co-founders and directors. I remember reading a couple of newspaper articles that inspired me, by David Weston[1] and Shaun Dellenty,[2] both of whom were "out" teachers for their own powerful reasons. I was inspired by them both to finally be "out" at work, and the strength of reaction showed me how necessary it was to continue working on LGBT+ visibility in schools. Without these two beacons of hope, LGBTed would not exist and nor would this book.

In two years, LGBTed has built a network of over 5,000 teachers and leaders, empowering us to be authentic in our schools, colleges and universities, to support our students and to be an advocate for increasing LGBT+ visibility in our education system. Like WomenEd and BAMEed, LGBTed is affecting real change in order to make schools more inclusive. Most recently, our *Proud Leadership* course, full funded by the Department for Education, has led to 75% of its participants achieving more responsibility or a promotion in their workplace.

It will use its links with universities to conduct and publish research into being "out" at work in schools and colleges; it will support and empower colleagues to come out at all levels in education; it will improve school leaders' knowledge of LGBT+ issues in education and will improve teacher retention by allowing colleagues to be more authentic in the workplace. LGBTed speak from experience: being a visible LGBT+ practitioner and witnessing the tangibly positive impact it has on young people is empowering, motivating and rewarding.

If there is any doubt as to why LGBT+ teachers and leaders *need* to be authentic in school, the statistics – where they exist – are scary. For example, let's take a look at the Stonewall School Report 2017[3]:

- Nearly half of LGB students are bullied at school, and 64% of trans students.
- Half of LGBT+ students hear homophobic language regularly in school.
- More than half of LGBT+ students feel that bullying has a negative effect on their education.
- Sixty-one per cent of LGBT+ young people have self-harmed.
- Forty-five per cent of young trans people have attempted to take their own life.
- Half of them have succeeded.
- Fifty-three per cent of LGBT+ students say there isn't an adult at their school they feel they can talk to.

For the sake of the young people that need us, this cannot continue. By having LGBT+ teachers and leaders who are authentic in the classroom, our young people will see it is possible to be successful and happy as an LGBT+ person. They will be reassured that there are other people out there who are different and are OK with it. For the purposes of this book, I wish to acknowledge the many different ways in which we "label" members of the LGBT+ community including LGBTQ+, LGBTQI+, LGBTQIA+ and the umbrella term "queer", all of which are considered to be acceptable. I personally prefer to use LGBT+, and we have chosen to use "LGBTed" for our organisation due to its simplicity.

Aside from being visible role models, there are lots more that teachers and leaders can do to support our LGBT+ students, and there will be examples throughout the chapters of this book. You could start by asking yourselves these questions:

### How often do you teach about LGBT+-related issues in your school?

In schools I have worked in, we have incorporated LGBT+ issues into a range of subjects for LGBT History Month, and the students found it incredibly enlightening. In Maths, they learned the heart-breaking story of Alan Turing. In Modern Foreign Languages (MFL), they learned all about the "secret" gay language of Polari. In Music, they learned about some of the most iconic music by LGBT+ artists before learning what they all had in common and discussing it. In Media Studies, they learned about the positive and negative representations of both sexuality and gender in music videos and were surprised by what they saw. In Geography, they learned about the huge number of countries that it is simply not safe to visit as an LGBT+ person, where LGBT+ people are tortured and killed simply for who they love. This was contrasted with liberal, welcoming British cities like Brighton, my beautiful home.

### What is your school's punishment for homophobic bullying?

You'd be surprised how many teachers don't know this when I have asked them. Obviously, all individual cases are different, but if this is not treated equally to racism, we are, again, failing young LGBT+ people.

### When have you intervened to stop or prevent homophobic bullying or homophobic language?

Homophobic language is often used casually (phrases such as "that's so gay" are still commonplace) and may be used more out of ignorance than out of malice, but is this being challenged and brought to young people's attention enough? There are thousands of other words that can be used, but they chose "gay". What does this say about their vocabulary? What is this saying to all those who are struggling to come to terms with their own sexuality?

### When have you missed an opportunity to support an LGBT+ student and what could you have done differently?

This might be the student who hangs around in your doorway and doesn't quite know how to say what they want to say to you; or this might be the student whose friends dismiss their name-calling as "banter". When teachers and leaders reflect honestly in my training sessions, I am told about so many examples where they feel they could have done more.

## Why the book title

I have been so grateful of many opportunities in the past few years to tell my story – at events, conferences, training sessions, and so forth. With my talk entitled *A Big Gay Adventure in*

*Education*, I have wanted to show people how this has been a positive, enlightening and fun journey for me. The focus on fun. Yes, there are many understandable fears and some perceived risks in being an "out" teacher, but this book intends to demonstrate how, in so many ways, being an "out" teacher is an overwhelmingly positive experience. A personal, powerful and professional one. It is an adventure. This book is not about me and my story is not unique. The many contributors to this book are breaking boundaries by sharing the adventures they have had as "out" teachers or as a student benefiting from one. With the title *Big Gay Adventures In Education*, it is my desire to remove the fear and the stigma that some might have about raising the issue and even about saying the "dreaded" g-word.

## Why come out

How do I respond to those who say "my sexuality has no place in the classroom"? Obviously, being "out" is a personal choice. But being a visible and authentic role model is not even about discussing your sexuality. It's not always assemblies and certainly isn't all jazz hands. It's having a picture of yourself with your same-sex partner on your desk in the classroom. It's mentioning your same-sex partner in conversation when asked by a student, without having to lie of self-mediate. It's being confident enough to bring your same-sex partner to sit with you in the audience at a school production. When a female colleague comes into school visibly pregnant, there is often an assumption made about her heterosexuality in our heteronormative world. Straight sexuality is represented all day every day. What is the equivalent for LGBT+ young people? We need to push for equity wherever we can find it. The LGBT+ young people will notice and they will appreciate it more than we'll know.

To those who say "you are not here to teach about sex" or "your sex lives should remain in the home", I say "who is talking about sex?" Talking about being gay is not talking about sex, in the same way that talking about your heterosexual wedding or talking about going for a walk at the weekend with your partner isn't talking about sex. In my experience, more often than not, it is the homophobes who bring it all back to sex. Mention you are gay and, out of the blue, they are the first to suddenly start talking about anal! They certainly appear to think about gay sex more than I ever do! I have never discussed my sex life with students, and it would never be appropriate to do so under any circumstances. Equally troubling is the argument that teaching about LGBT+ issues isn't "age appropriate". What is not "age appropriate" about knowing that a man can marry a man and a woman can marry a woman when they are in love? What is not "age appropriate" about knowing some children have two dads or two mums, in the same way that some have only one parent or none at all? It is certainly "age appropriate" for those students who live the experience every day. We cannot allow some young people to feel that their existence is any less valid. This is what destroys lives. And with the statutory sex education guidelines recently changing, this book is more timely and relevant than ever.

Finally, what about those who say "you are here to teach about the curriculum, get on with your job"? To them I say simply this: without feeling welcome, safe and secure, LGBT+ students won't see any point in accessing a curriculum.

With this book I want to bring everybody on board for the benefit of the LGBT+ young people who need us. Often, judgements are made against our "movement" through fear:

fear of the unknown, fear of upsetting the status quo, fear of losing an assumed level of "privilege". Therefore, I have tried to present this book in a way that alleviates those fears. I have been fortunate to meet some genuinely inspirational people on my adventure, all of whom demonstrate in this book that there is little to be scared of. These people range from trainee teachers to experienced school leaders across the LGBT+ spectrum. There are even some examples from LGBT+ students whose lives were made better by having an openly LGBT+ teacher. What you'll see in this book is how much we all have in common: all of the stories in this collection are lived experiences, positive experiences, shared by one human being with another. LGBT+ teachers can hopefully learn from this, but more importantly, we need heterosexual allies if we are ever to reach a place where all LGBT+ young people can feel safe and included in their school communities. But this book is not just for teachers. It is my hope that parents, families, corporations and many others will gain something from it, whether it is practical advice, a feeling of empowerment or a sense of solidarity. We have all been to school, we all remember the variety of experiences we had, why not make them better for those who follow?

There are thousands of children who still experience what I did at school but suffer in silence. Some have since entered the teaching profession, like me, to right these wrongs. A small number are also openly LGBT+ including one I recently spoke to who is beginning his first placement as an "out" teacher because of what I did. This is my message to everyone: come and join me on a big gay adventure in education and let's be the role models we needed when we were at school.

## Notes

1 Now CEO of Teacher Development Trust and co-author of *Unleashing Great Teaching* (2018) with Bridget Clay.
2 Now author of *Celebrating Difference: A Whole School Approach to LGBT+ Inclusion* (2019).
3 https://www.stonewall.org.uk/system/files/the_school_report_2017.pdf

# 2 To be out or not to be out
*Sue Sanders*

*Legendary lesbian Sue Sanders is a teacher, equalities trainer and a member of several independent advisory groups to the Criminal Justice System. She is also co-founder of the UK LGBT History Month and co-ordinator of OUTing the Past, the biggest lesbian, gay, bisexual and trans (LGBT) history festival in the UK. In this chapter, Sue writes about being an "out" lesbian during a time when lesbian, gay, bisexual, trans and others (LGBT+) people were mostly invisible and how she used her experiences to improve the lives of others.*

To be out or not to be out depends on so many factors. Safety is a big issue. I do not take for granted that as a white, middle-class, educated woman, I have certain privileges. Those privileges give me responsibilities. I want to use them so I can be out where it might be hard for others.

Professionally it has taken me some time to say, "Hello I am Sue Sanders; I'm a lesbian!" In my last year at Drama college, in the late 1960s, I finally came out to myself fully and to the whole college. I did this in anger as much as anything else because I was so frustrated that it had taken me so long to find another lesbian.

## 1970s education jobs

In my first teaching job in an all-girls school, I found it impossible to play the subterfuge game and as a motorbike-riding, trouser, shirt and comfortable-shoes wearing, woman with no makeup, I was hardly "passing"! In the late 1960s and early 1970s, LGBT people were dealing with the fact that we were invisible. The stereotypes of homosexuals were that we were pathetic or predatory and that we lived in a twilight world. I wanted sunshine and honesty and wanted to prove to myself and others that the stereotypes were not true. I was partially out, and I did not wear badges as I do today; I probably did not describe myself as a lesbian, but people knew I lived with a very butch looking woman, as our flat was near the school. It was known and not known, a tacit understanding.

I was out in a similar sort of way to the drama Inspectors of the Inner London Education Authority (ILEA) who offered me a job in a Further Education College. This at a time when some gay male teachers were getting the sack when it became known they were homosexual. I was soon more at home in the mainly adult environment and could be open with both students and staff. I was often to be found smoking a coloured pipe that matched my trousers in the staffroom!

I moved to Australia in 1975 and taught at teacher training establishments. I was more circumspect then as I was living with a well-known artist who was married and firmly in the closet. She felt she had to be "careful of her reputation". At work, I was pioneering the whole concept of drama as a subject that could be used to enable students to become more confident and express their whole selves. I was not "passing", my wardrobe had not changed. I was simply not open about my orientation.

Once I began teaching in the women's prison however, things changed. I have no idea if the civil servant in the Corrective Services, a man, who gave me the job knew I was lesbian, but I did not come out to him. He wanted me to be involved in the prison, as he saw the potential of rehabilitation through drama, after reading an article I had written on the subject. I set up a course in drama and creative writing for the prisoners. The lesbian warders and I recognised each other. The prisoners knew and had no problems.

Meanwhile, I applied to teach at a Catholic Girls' school. The Mother Superior hired me as soon as I told her I was already teaching in the women's prison. The staff, a mixture of nuns and civvies, were accepting of me. Again, I was obvious but not strident. I had an idea that if the girls developed a drama piece based on the writings on the women in the prison, I might arrange a performance in the prison, giving the girls the experience of performance, introducing them to the women inmates and helping the prisoners to see the value of their creative work. The school and warden agreed.

On the day I brought the show to the prison, the warders, who disliked me, were wearing broad smiles as they herded the reluctant, frowning women into the room that was to be our theatre. Why did they have to watch this play put on by middle-class children who meant nothing to them personally? They had no choice but to be there. Once the play started and the women heard their own words and sentiments on exploring freedom and power, they loved the show and enthusiastically applauded the girls. As their smiles grew, so the warders' smiles were replaced with scowls. The warders threatened to go on strike if I was not sacked. They claimed I was encouraging masturbatory and lesbian practices, and the irony was not lost on me!

## 1970s and 1980s theatre work

One would think working in theatre would be easier as an "out" lesbian, but in both Sydney and London, my experiences were not always "happy". In Sydney, I was the Education officer at the Seymour Centre (the Sydney University Theatre), where I authored and pioneered teaching packs that linked the secondary school curriculum to plays we were staging, for example, the original Australian play, "A Hard God", by Peter Kenna. I was out to Centre staff and the schools I worked with. My one-year contract was not extended. The cost of being "out"? We are never sure.

I worked at the ABC where I researched, produced and presented programmes that explored two themes, Women and Madness, and Women in Prison over three programmes. They were explicit about the homophobia of the prison staff, many of whom were closeted lesbians.

On returning to the UK in 1979, I became the co-ordinator of the Oval House Theatre, on the London Fringe in Lambeth. It was well known for staging new and politically challenging work. Although I put on LGB plays that were successful at our box office, I was not encouraged and discovered in the first year that management was not my forte.

I worked successfully as a freelance director with amongst others the Scarlet Harlots Theatre Company and Siren Theatre Company, and joined "Women in Entertainment", a community education and campaigning project. We ran a series of workshops on the use of drama in youth work for women youth workers. We challenged the dearth of black women, disabled women and lesbians in the theatre in general.

## 1980s and Section 28

Working as a supply teacher through the 1980s and 1990s was a mixed bag. I clocked the potential "friends of Dorothy" in the staffroom, but more often than not they avoided me. They perceived me as a threat to their "safe closets".

When the tory government proposed Section 28 in their Local Authorities Bill (LA Bill), to discourage the acceptance of LGBT families, teachers who were "in" became even more nervous. I was past caring about my safety and my privilege did protect me. I became a vocal and public fighter of the bill, was interviewed by journalists on television and radio and joined the Education and Arts Lobbies. I was working with Ian Mckellen and Michael Cashman in the latter, alongside less well-known figures like theatre critic, Carol Woddis, and the Director of the Drill Hall, Julie Parker.

In the Education Lobby, Paul Patrick, an out teacher in South East London, and I, teamed up. We were both National Union of Teachers (NUT [now National Education Union]) members, and we encouraged the union to recognise the plight of its Lesbian and Gay members and then offer them support. Paul and I, both drama teachers, passionate about how poetry, plays and the theatre can instigate positive change, formed a bond, a working partnership. Throughout the time of Section 28 and beyond, we devised and delivered training for the Public and Voluntary sector on Equality and Diversity with the focus on Lesbian and Gay issues. We were out, proud and ... loud. Schools Out UK – of which Paul and I were members, and then became co-chairs – campaigned against Section 28. We plotted strategies and held annual conferences for LGBT teachers and their allies. They were uplifting affairs with teachers coming together sharing their ideas, talking about being out or dealing with being in the closet. Celebrities like Ian McKellen, Cyril Nri and Mz Fontaine, now Chaune King, came and inspired us. We were very grateful for their involvement.

Paul and I were out, and some teachers and students, as I said, had a problem with that. What is heartening (and what I have found through my life) is that while some people have expressed anger and disgust at me, and perhaps distance themselves. Given time, some have mellowed and come to accept and even acknowledge it in themselves. That is worth remembering when you get a jibe thrown at you. If you can stay true and strong, you will find some people change their minds, and even apologise, as they realise how wrong or defensive they have been.

Although the LA Bill was passed and made the law of the land, it had an unintended consequence. An LGBT Campaigning Community was formed to fight for our human rights. It was as if we woke up to our responsibility and power.

## 1990s expanding the campaign

Hate crime, however, is a different matter, and I joined a group in Southwark, who were working with the council and police to tackle homophobic crime. Victims of racist and/or homophobic crime frequently do not report. They have little or no faith that the police will care, having often seen both racist and homophobic police behaviour.

In Southwark, I wanted to use my personal knowledge and experience to help educate the Council and local police. A group of Southwark residents, all out lesbians and gays formed the Anti-Homophobic Forum and had the credibility of experience when deciding strategies to tackle the rampant homophobia of the day. Attacks were happening; we knew it from a survey we commissioned in 2001. It provided statistics and anecdotal evidence. Section 28 had sanctioned and encouraged the prejudice that fuelled the onslaught of 1999, when a lone bomber attacked Brixton, Brick Lane and finally The Admiral Duncan. He proved what we had been saying that we had to tackle all hate crime, as it is all linked. The perpetrator was found and prosecuted. He wanted to attack African Caribbean people in Brixton, Asians in Brick lane and then LGBT in the Admiral Duncan. Of course, all their friends and allies were targeted and victimised as well.

## 2000s training the criminal justice system

After the Steven Lawrence Inquiry, I helped deliver its recommended Equality and Anti-Racism training to the criminal justice system (the police, Crown Prosecution Service (CPS) and parts of the Judiciary). I was hired by the consultancy assigned to deliver the training, after convincing them that it was crucial to include anti-homophobia in the training. Here again, being out was crucial part of my credibility. We delivered the training in pairs that modelled diversity. I worked with a Black or Asian person, usually a man. Most ethnic minority people have no choice but to be "out" as to their colour. As a white woman, I could bring a valuable perspective to the need for tackling racism. When I came out as a lesbian, as I always did, another issue entered the room.

The atmosphere could be very confrontational from the police, as they were required to attend the sessions, and thus, some felt they were accused of being "racist" and/or "homophobic". It was often a delicate process to enable them to recognise we were there to help them to be more professional in dealing with the public and we had personal knowledge we could use to demonstrate the changes that were needed.

Coming back from one of those courses, I was asked by a taxi driver in the casual way they do, "What have you been doing today?" It may not surprise you that I did not always say, "Oh, I have been training the police about dealing effectively with racism and homophobia." I have learnt that it is wise to choose my moments and know that an argument in a cab may not be a good use of my energy. Having said that, I can remember some very positive reactions when I have had the energy to be forth coming.

Being "out" can be draining, dangerous and exhausting but exhilarating. Having a "safe space" to come home to is crucial. My partner of over 30 years, Jeanne Nadeau, has helped provide that space. Her experience as a management consultant and pyschotherapist has been invaluable. We have, in that time, written together, trained together, supported each other's work and explored theories and politics. We have navigated domestic and public issues of visibility and invisibility.

Professionally now, I am fully out. As the chair of Schools Out UK, the co-founder of LGBT History Month with Paul Patrick (b. 1950, d. 2008) and the founder of The Classroom website, "out" is a given.

When Stuart Milk, the nephew of Harvey Milk, awarded me an Emeritus Professorship of the Harvey Milk Institute, it meant a great deal to me on so many counts. I am not an academic, and I failed my 11 plus and got 0 level passes for my A levels. I had refused the chance to be given any awards as they had the word "empire" in them. Harvey was famous for encouraging people to come out and to give people hope, two things I am passionate about.

I helped to set up the first Independent LGBT Advisory Group (IAG) in a democratic and inclusive way. We worked within Scotland Yard. I have also been involved in IAGs to the CPS and the ECHR and supported the team that dealt with the Paddington rail disaster of 1999. In all these roles, it is essential that I am "out" and my experience is mostly welcomed and listened to, if not always acted on. It is a crying shame that the Department for Education (DfE) has rarely asked for it. Meanwhile, many local authorities and Non-Governmental Organisations have availed themselves of my freelance training practice and relied on my knowledge and experience of being an out lesbian.

Schools need to be a microcosm of society, so students can meet representatives of the whole population. A good school will prepare its students by having a diverse staff who are their authentic selves. They will therefore make sure their LGBT staff, be they cleaners, cooks, caretakers, office workers or teachers, are welcome and enabled to be "out" if they so wish. The Equality Act of 2010 and the Public Sector Equality Duty as well as the new Relationships and Sex Education (RSE) syllabus mean that teachers from all the protected characteristics are acknowledged for having much to offer.

In disenabling teachers to be out, they are disenabled to be fully effective teachers. The amount of energy wasted in hiding can be immense, and teaching, I would argue, demands you are full of energy and open about your whole self. Otherwise, vital role models are lost. Students will receive a very powerful subliminal message that if you are not white, able-bodied, heterosexual and Christian, you have little or no place in society.

If a teacher is not out, then the students are free to assume, learn or believe, at a very basic level, that there is something wrong with being LGBT+. We owe it to our students to work towards making every school a safe space for all LGBT+ people, students, parents, teachers and all other staff.

## Big gay notes from the editor

*Sue's advice that "if you can stay true and strong, you will find some people can change their minds" accurately upholds why this book exists. LGBT+ people are here and are not going away; we should bring people with us – as she has always aimed to do – and not alienate them.*

*Many LGBT+ people have shared experiences of colleagues who avoid them because they feel them to be a threat to their "safety" of privilege in their schools. Many LGBT+ teachers I have spoken to have not come out because they are worried about the rejection and discrimination they may face as a result.*

*I have much admiration for what Sue has achieved through her lived experiences and how she has been a genuine trailblazer. She agrees that, if an LGBT+ teacher is not "out", they are invisible. Consequently, students learn at a very basic level there is something wrong with being LGBT+. Without positive LGBT+ role models, we will not be able to kill off the vile stereotypes of gay people being either pathetic or predatory. More examples of visible LGBT+ role models will follow throughout this book.*

# 3 It's OK
## A school assembly

*David Lowbridge-Ellis*

*David Lowbridge-Ellis is a deputy headteacher from the West Midlands. He leads on lesbian, gay, bisexual, trans and others (LGBT+) inclusion as a visible LGBT+ role model in the school where he has worked for 15 years. He has delivered many workshops for LGBTed and other organisations to share good practice for 'queering' the curriculum in all subject areas. In this chapter, he shares the transcript for a very personal and empowering assembly he delivered in his school to support LGBT+ young people.*

When I was at school, this assembly would have been illegal. I'll explain why in a minute.

There are two words I want you to remember from today's assembly. Technically it's three words because one of them is joined to another with an apostrophe. Sorry, I'm quite pedantic about these things. I am an English teacher after all.

But the words you need to remember are these:

It's OK.

That's it. That's all I need you to remember. Two – or three – words. They don't sound very powerful, do they? But I promise you: if you remember them, you can change the world.

Don't believe me?

Well, when I was at school, in the 1980s and 1990s, none of my teachers could say those words. They were forbidden, by law.

Yes, they could say 'it's OK' to one of my classmates if they fell over and hurt their knee. They could make them feel better until the pain went away. And believe me: I know what that sort of pain feels like. I fell over a lot in the playground when I was at school. My trousers always had patches over the knees.

My teachers could also say 'it's OK' to one of us if a pet had died. I remember when my goldfish breathed his last underwater breath. I held a big funeral for him in the back garden. And for a week of school, all I wrote about was my goldfish. Every Monday morning, our teachers had us 'write about what you did at the weekend', probably because they wanted a few quiet minutes to get setup for the week ahead. I wrote about the burial my whole family had given my goldfish the day before. Five days later, on Friday afternoon, I still wasn't finished grieving for my goldfish. We were tasked with writing poems. With this particular teacher I had an ongoing … shall we say 'friendly disagreement' about whether poems had to rhyme. I was adamant: it wasn't a poem unless it rhymed. I must have been around eight or nine. I was stubborn even then. I still remember racking my brain for words that rhymed with 'fish'. I couldn't think of many, and the ones I didn't come up with, 'dish' and 'squish', weren't exactly appropriate for eulogising the loss of my pet.

Of course, now I realise this teacher was right: poems don't always have to rhyme. Children don't know everything. It's true. I know you don't believe me, but it is. And one day, you will look back and go 'Mr Lowbridge-Ellis was right about this thing I was certain he was wrong about'. Sometimes we don't like to have our minds changed about things. It's human nature. The best we can do as teachers is present you with the facts.

Unfortunately, my teachers could not always do that. They were not allowed to.

When I was at school, there was a law in place that stopped our teachers telling us some very important facts, for instance, when someone on the playground described something as 'gay' when it was nothing of the sort.

Now I know that you would be shocked if one of your teachers overheard someone saying something that was clearly wrong and didn't correct them. Imagine if someone in your class said that 2 + 2 = 5 and your maths teacher just ignored it, or even agreed with that person. Or the person sitting next to you in science said that the world was flat and your science teacher did not pause to point out the truth: that it's round.

You would be just as shocked as if you heard someone say 'that's so gay' and your teacher did nothing to correct that person's mistake.

We are a proudly diverse school. That means we don't make other people feel rubbish about themselves, however different they may be to us. It's why we don't describe things as 'gay' when really we mean 'it's a bit rubbish'.

When I was at school, it was very different. Everything was 'gay'. A piece of really boring homework no one wanted to do: *This geography homework is so gay*. An own goal in football: *That goal was sooooo gay*. A pair of trainers from a brand that wasn't in fashion. My parents didn't believe in buying me Adidas or Nike. They said people just paid for the brand name. I disagreed. That's another thing I'll now happily admit I was wrong about. Back then though, I was mortified. I had trainers with 'Hi-Tec' written on them. According to lots of people in my PE class, they were *well gay*.

It sounds daft when you stop to think about it, doesn't it? How can a pair of trainers be gay? Or an unfortunate goal? Or a piece of homework?

Everything was gay but not a lot actually was gay, in its true meaning anyway. In fact, the only thing that I knew was truly gay was me.

Can you imagine what it's like being described as 'rubbish' everyday? It doesn't make you feel great I can tell you.

So I grew up thinking being gay was a bad thing, that there was something very wrong with me. And other people thought there must be something wrong with me too. Of course, I know now another thing I didn't know then: the truth about bullies. The truth is they want to make other people feel bad because they feel really bad about themselves. And someone who feels like they're rubbish will always be able to find something about someone else they don't like. You'd think I was bullied enough just for having ginger hair, or Hi-Tec trainers, but being gay on top of this meant I was bullied *a lot*.

All it needed was one of my teachers, like your teachers would if it ever happened here, to step in and say THIS IS NOT OK: You can't keep using the word 'gay' in the wrong way. You can't bully people because they are a bit different to you. You'd call them out on it. Just like we all would if someone bullied someone with different coloured skin. I know that everyone in here would do this. You would challenge it yourself or tell a teacher. My school was not like this one. The fact is that no school was when it came to homophobia.

I said that this assembly would have been illegal when I was at school and it's true. My teachers weren't allowed to say anything – by law. They were told by the government that they weren't allowed to 'promote' homosexuality, which is kind of ridiculous when you think about it. It's like people thought it was a disease other people might catch, or it was like in Star Wars when Darth Vader tries to tempt Luke Skywalker into joining the dark side.

Now your science teachers can tell you why this is complete nonsense. Or you can learn from Lady Gaga. You may be too young to know who she is … How many of you have heard of Lady Gaga? Anyone not with their hand up has a bit of homework to do. It's an essential part of your education. Look up a song called Born This Way on Spotify or YouTube, and you'll learn everything you need to about why being queer isn't a choice.

I like the term 'queer' more than 'LGBT' which you may have also heard of. When I was at school, 'queer' was used as an offensive word, but now we use it to include all sexual orientations and gender identities, including lesbian, gay, bisexual, transgender, non-binary, asexual, pansexual and others. 'Queer' is what's known as an umbrella term, because lots of people who feel different get to stand underneath it and use it to refer to each other. And even if you're not queer but you're what's called an ally, you can stand with queer people. It's a bit like the Rihanna song. If you treat everyone with respect, you can stand under this umbrella (ella ella).

Of course, lots have changed since I was at school, a long time ago, in a galaxy not that far away …

But it's a mistake to think that this is all just history and everything is fine now. In 70 countries around the world, it's still illegal to be gay. Even in this country, almost all queer young are bullied at some point in their school lives. Horribly, 25% of young queer people attempt to end their own lives. And nearly a quarter of homeless people identify as queer.

So what can we all do? We can say what my teachers were never allowed to say. Those two – or three – words: IT'S OK.

IT'S OK to be gay. IT'S OK to be lesbian. IT'S OK to be bi, or somewhere in between straight and gay. IT'S OK if you don't feel like a girl or a boy, whatever happens to be written on your birth certificate. IT'S OK if you don't feel much or any attraction at all. IT'S OK to love whoever you want.

Whoever you are, my best friend or just someone I sit next to in maths, IT'S OK.

I don't want anyone in here to go through what I went through at school. But even more than that, I want you to be the people to make the world a better place for all queer people. One day, we won't need assemblies like this. We won't need Pride parades. We won't need rainbow flags. It won't happen overnight. But one day, maybe when I'm old and wrinkly, I will be able to walk down the street holding my husband's hand, and it will feel different. Picture us: the wrinkly old Lowbridge-Ellises doddering down to the shops. We'll be there, holding our wrinkly hands together, and we'll realise we're not afraid anymore. We'll realise we're not worried about people saying things to us, or doing things to us, just because we're showing each other affection.

You are the people who will make this happen. Let's start today, by making sure everyone hears this loud and clear: IT'S OK.

## Big gay notes from the editor

*Many of the chapters in this book are accounts of how assemblies have worked well to get a consistent message across, showing LGBT+ young people they are welcome in the school. There are, of course, many other ways to do this, and there is no 'correct' way to 'come out' due to it being such a personal matter.*

*David, like Sue Sanders in the previous chapter, speaks poignantly about what I call the 'homophobic hangover' left in schools by the Section 28 legislation. He communicates his message in a student-friendly manner so that young people can know the history of LGBT+ rights and how we got here today. When teaching any aspect of civil rights or equality, it is important not to underestimate the extent of the prejudice that has been faced for decades.*

*Throughout his work, David leads by example and shows us that LGBT+ issues in schools are not a 'one-off' event but must be seen as part of the curriculum intent, implementation and impact in order to affect real change. Only by doing this can we untangle the toxic legacy of Section 28 at its roots.*

# 4 Miss, are you a lesbian?
## Becoming bisexual

*Adele Bates*

*Adele Bates is an educator and advocator for inclusion in education and students with Social, Emotional and Mental Health needs. With over 18 years' experience, Adele teaches these pupils in a variety of educational settings and also trains others to do so. She was a TEDx Speaker 2020 and the author of the Behaviour Guide 'Miss, I don't give a sh\*t' with Sage Publications. In this chapter, Adele recounts how discovering her sexuality has been a journey, familiar to many, and the importance of bi-visibility in schools.*

> PUPIL[1]:   Miss, are you a Lesbian?
> ME:        No, Bisexual (we were in a minibus, I had time…)
> PUPIL:     You're greedy
> ME:        Why do you think that?
> PUPIL:     Because you can go out with everyone!
> ME:        I'm actually going to marry one person
> PUPIL:     OK then

I first began teaching when I was 16 years old. I ran a local drama school for primary school aged children, I put them through exams, they won placements and festivals and we put on many a show. Since then, I have worked in mainstream primary, secondary and infant schools, PRUs, APs, schools for pupils with profound disabilities, and I have lectured at Universities.

At the time of writing, I am 34 years old.

When I was 16 years old I was straight.

When I was 27 years old I discovered I wasn't; I fell in love.

This person happened to be a different shape in their pants to all the other people I had dated previously. She is a woman – she's also Eastern European which brings a whole other bag of fun, but that's for a different time…

Since my journey began into 'becoming a bisexual' there have been a variety of uniquely weird moments:

- being shocked on our second date when I nipped to the loo only to find my date was following me in
- upsetting moments – when I realised Disney no longer represented me
- awkward moments as I discovered (probably unsurprisingly if I'd thought about it) that lesbian porn is also entirely inaccurate

- sad moments – as I found out that some close family and friends actually did have problems with 'my change'
- lonely moments – as well-meaning straight friends and misunderstanding gay friends revealed that I had no one close to talk to about 'the transition'
- scary moments – when I dared to hold hands with my girlfriend in front of Bulgarian policemen with guns
- positive moments – when I started getting a flood of work from my new lesbian community and contacts
- difficult moments – including spouts of lesbian, gay, bisexual and trans (LGBT)-ignorance or phobia *during* a smear test
- and many amusing moments – such as accidentally coming on to a female friend over text or finding myself having to reassure an ex-boyfriend that this had nothing to do with our previous sex life

Underlying all this is a struggle with the gay/lesbian/straight/bi/+ labels and a self-acceptance of what, or rather whom, makes me happy now, and daring myself to be brave enough to follow that love.

Then there was my teaching…

Only a year after finding my now-fiancée, I decided to re-focus my career and make teaching the main part (before this I was mainly an opera singer who taught performing arts). Having always taught freelance, it was time to get the PGCE under my belt and I chose English to make me more employable (plus, I just couldn't bring myself to teach 30+ teenagers with recorders, or probably ukuleles now). Through the application process it began to dawn on me – I would be perceived to be a 'gay' teacher. It was strange. In the theatre world it was positively normal to be surrounded by a whole host of sexualities and gender-identities, I had been privileged and fortunate enough to never have to hide my sexuality at work. How would that work in schools?

My first litmus test was the interviews.

During the interview with my soon-to-be course tutor, Dr Steve Roberts, he asked what I was currently reading. I'm always reading around seven books at a time, so could have chosen any – including the ones I was reading about teaching! Instead, instinctively I felt I wanted to test something. I told him: *The Well of Loneliness, Radclyffe Hall*. Steve didn't miss a beat, not only had he heard of this Western Lesbian Classic, he had also read it. I was safe.

But I *had* needed to test, in a way my previously straight safe wouldn't have had to.

This was the beginning of many lesbian, gay, bisexual, trans and others (LGBT+) safety tests for me in education.

Student reading the latest Captain Underpants books:
The two main characters George and Harold travel in a time machine and meet their future selves:
They meet George, his wife and children.
They meet Harold, his husband and children.
My student said 'Oooo gay' and carried on reading.

Amid the usual PGCE madness, I got asked to teach a form group on Anti-Bullying week. I asked the teacher I was working with if the work covered LGBT+ bullying. She told me that it touched upon it, but that *'you should be careful teaching that because we think H might be gay.'* I genuinely had no idea what she meant by that: don't teach anti-bullying because someone might be gay? It took me several months to realise, that rather than helpful mentoring advice, this was in fact a display of the teacher's own lack of knowledge and ignorance around LGBT+ issues. Needless to say, I took that as a challenge to in fact make sure that LGBT+ bullying was *definitely* a part of that lesson, and that H – or anyone else who happened to be there, knew where specific LGBT+ support could be found.

But the moment was coming, I could feel it, when I would have to 'out' myself to the students.

Now it is not of course compulsory to be out with students. It is each individual's choice; however, I had never been 'in' in the first place. I had *never once* hidden the gender of my partner to students, when I was straight, and in general I am a pretty open teacher, to hide my female partner, would be like trying to hide that I live in a flat. To do so, just because she happens to be a different gender to the others made me feel sick. I was beginning to learn what it meant to be in a minority. As a white, cis-gender, English speaking woman in England, I had never felt this before; I had my first big PGCE meltdown.

The madness of it was, despite being nearly 30, an independent, confident woman who knew her own identity and place in the world, with a loving family and accepting society – I *still* felt like it was me making too much of a fuss. Like I was wrong for feeling so displaced, that I was wrong for questioning and correcting the teachers who were trying to support me, like I was wrong to suddenly be angry at Margaret Thatcher when I realised that I had been a child of Section 28, like I was wrong to be thinking about this so much when there were Teaching Standards to prove and detentions to follow up- and all of it made me realise how difficult it must be for my LGBT+ students who didn't have all the advantages I had as an adult who could make my own choices – plus my hormones were probably a little more stable than theirs.

Luckily my instincts with my tutor Steve had been right. I spent a good two hours or so in his office using up his tissues. Luckily for me he got it. He has in-direct experience of LGBT+ issues close to him; he got my struggle. From this conversation he instigated a group for all PGCE trainees at the University who wanted to discuss/find support in being an LGBT+ teacher. I believe in consecutive years this support has been offered before first placement.

Scene during my first placement -

| | |
|---|---|
| PUPIL: | I went go-karting last week. |
| ME: | Oh really? My partner did that recently, she loved it. |
| PUPIL: | Your partner's a *she*? |
| ME: | *(heart in throat)* yes. |
| PUPIL: | *(pauses for a very long time)* I would have thought your partner would be a *he*. |
| ME: | Well some people have *hes* and some people have *shes* (sorry, was too nervous at this point to add non-binary genders). |
| PUPIL: | *(pauses again for an even longer time. Thinking)* Miss T my form tutor had a partner, she was crying yesterday because he dumped her. |
| ME: | *(I have no recollection of what I taught for the rest of that lesson).* |

During my second placement the stakes got higher.

I experienced an incident of homophobic/biphobic abuse from a member of the public during a school trip. While on the trip a member of the public expressed his disgust at homosexual people, and when I told him (possibly unwisely, my fiancée is quite scared I'll get thumped one day soon) that I had a girlfriend, he went on to discuss his lesbian sexual threesome fantasies – in front of the pupils!

I was shaken and disturbed, and quickly took the pupils away. However, as a PGCE trainee – where most days seem stressful and overwhelming – I didn't think any further action would happen. I am part of the LGBT+ community and this, I was learning, happens to us. Regularly.

I mentioned the incident as a part of reflection in my mentor meeting. My mentor, a Lead Practitioner for English – Paul Offord, took this up immediately. His training and knowledge of the discrimination policies within school, and the school's duty in protecting me while at work, meant that suddenly I didn't have to bear this alone. I attended three meetings with senior management to discuss the incident. On behalf of me, the school contacted the local business association, of which this person was an employee, and the police. The association added a section in their newsletter on their responsibility as public businesses on upholding the Equality Act. I had an interview with the police, who visited the business and spoke to the manager and gentleman concerned, and Paul regularly checked to ensure that the incident had not affected me in any other adverse way. This was exemplary practice: the school valued my contribution and supported me with discrimination.

Since these fledgling years of full-time teaching and sexual orientation exploration I have become, thanks to colleagues – both LGBT+ and straight and cis allies, increasingly comfortable as an out Bi teacher. I also did the Amnesty International Teacher Training and was privileged enough to meet the fabulous Shaun Dellenty several times – who I absolutely can't help fan-girling *every* time. I still must test, though now – understanding my rights and laws much more intricately – I test to ensure that schools are upholding exemplary practice rather than if I am going to be accepted. I took on the Lead on Equality and Diversity in one school, have delivered LGBT+ training to colleagues and trainees, assemblies on LGBT+ issues and human rights have written many articles on LGBT+ education. At one stage I was tinkering with making LGBT+ awareness in schools my main focus, but decided that in the UK there are already many fantastic people leading this work. Instead I focus on inclusion in another area – students with SEMH and Behaviour issues, another group of vulnerable young people who have often experienced trauma, abuse and neglect – and yet are discriminated and even *excluded* from our society. The parallels and crossover with our LGBT+ students is clear.

The best thing about feeling safe enough to be an out Bi teacher is the role modelling. Every day that I get to teach authentically, and as Frederic Laloux says 'take my whole self to work', I am sending a message to our young people: it's OK to be you too, however you are different. I've supported many LGBT+ young people as they've come out, questioned, told their parents – the my most humbling memory is being the first adult a trans student told about their gender identity. In my current work now, mostly in PRUs and APs with many excluded students, I also get the chance to have these discussions with them – and nearly every time they bowl me over with their acceptance and love, when they often come from such difficult situations themselves.

Message in a Christmas card from a pupil:

'To Miss Bates and her girlfriend'

I cried for hours.

## Big gay notes from the editor

*A key take-away from this chapter is, if you are an ally of the LGBT+ community or an LGBT+ leader, it is incredibly helpful to make yourself known to other LGBT+ colleagues. This might be as simple as wearing a rainbow badge or lanyard, or by taking the time to refer openly to LGBT+ inclusion in your school policy. This enables us to have a shared experience and to know that we can air our views and concerns in a safe space. Some headteachers have told me they have displayed the LGBTed logo on their website and direct feedback has shown this has helped with recruiting a more diverse team, including teachers who may not have felt comfortable applying otherwise. With each opportunity to be our authentic selves, we become more comfortable to promote inclusivity for others.*

*The idea that a teacher should be 'careful' teaching about LGBT+ issues because a student might be gay is somewhat baffling and it was down to Adele's own courage and determination to contradict this advice that she has undoubtedly made a difference for the students she teachers. In particular, the touching responses from her more challenging children demonstrates that the children we teach benefit from seeing their teachers as human beings, and it can of course be the more challenging students that often need us most. Bi-visibility, in particular, is lacking in schools and this is the first of several chapters exploring this issue.*

## Note

1 Most of the pupils in this story are in Pupil Referral Units or Alternative Provision Schools. Many have been excluded from several other schools due to behaviour.

# 5 Out from the outset
*Kip Webb-Heller*

*Kip Webb-Heller is a trans, non-binary, queer trainee teacher. They are motivated by inclusion and hope to use their experiences as a queer person, an art specialist and a Jew to make a difference to the world. They live with their fiancé and dog near Brighton. In this chapter they offer their unique perspective on their teacher training as an "out" trans teacher from the very beginning, the impact this had on them as an individual and on the young people they taught.*

I made a very conscious decision to be as out as possible from the moment I started my teacher training degree.

At age 20, I came to university from a pretty tense family environment. That summer, I had told my family I intended to physically transition. I had been as open as I could with them about my gender identity over the previous years – though as I'm sure most queer people have experienced, the process we have to go through to understand and accept ourselves in our own heads is a huge one, before we can ever verbalise it to others. By this point I was familiar with confusion and erasure of my gender identity: "everyone is a man or a woman, non-binary is made up", "transtrenders", "I'm not going to call you 'they' because I don't like the grammar", "yes, but your body is female," and "how can you say you're a 'he' and a 'they'? You're confused!" I had previously worked in dance, and – whilst the arts may be a more progressive place for many things – binary, deterministic and often clichéd views of gender still fed into almost every experience I had, bubbling away just under the surface.

My family were no different to the rest of the world in this, but I was OK with it taking time and patience. No one is born educated on gender matters, and we all carry our own internalised shame, confusion and misconceptions. However, when I told my family that I was going to physically transition at some point (I was only on an infamously long waiting list for a Gender Identity Clinic by then), the result was explosive and revealed rejection of my autonomy to identify how I did and own my physical existence in the world.

I explain this because, like all lesbian, gay, bisexual, trans and others (LGBT+) teachers, it's important to know where I came from when entering the teaching world. Teaching is the career I am pursuing in many parts *because* of my experiences and existence as a trans person. Whilst I carry pain and remnants of shame that I have not managed to work through yet, it seems vital to me that I do not hide my identity – especially as an educator. I am motivated by the thought of making a difference to the world, of being a role model, of challenging the status quo. Accepting how (very) trans I was and deciding to go into teaching were linked processes. It had been tough reaching that point especially because I had had no visible role models, especially because my identity wasn't acknowledged even as a possibility when I was in school and especially because I had gone so far in my life following paths I believed I had to follow because of the body parts I had and because it made people around me happy. I desperately needed to shatter those blind expectations we put on children – be it well-meaning or not.

Looking back, I internalised so many messages about gender from everybody around me. There were plenty of throwaway, negative comments about queer people that those who said them barely even thought about. But more insidiously entering my subconscious was the praise and love I received according to how well I performed the gender I had been assigned. Most people were not trying to be harmful, but from so many different angles, I was given the same message. The fairy tales and books I read, the films I watched, the songs I heard – most contained highly gendered instructions about how to be a boy or a girl. I would hear from other children that something was just for girls, another just for boys. They in turn had heard it from siblings, parents or wider society. Adults around me reinforced what I was learning in their behaviour towards themselves and others. Activities I took part in became increasingly gender-exclusive as I got older. Different things were expected of me – then perceived as a girl – and my friends who were boys at school – sometimes that felt advantageous and sometimes it felt so unfair. As my interests and preferences developed, I remember feeling intensely frustrated that people assumed I liked or wouldn't like certain things. It felt so limiting, but as an obedient and anxious child, I found it too overwhelming to tackle head-on. I began to work just as hard but more quietly, finding it was confirmed to me many times over that I was not someone who made sense to others. I felt I was broken, or an alien, and grappled with depression from age ten. I feel I often still get overlooked because of the tendency I developed towards hiding myself away. I found that my way to cope was to play the long game and prove my ability through actions and eventual achievements – but this was a lot of pressure on young shoulders.

Maybe some people would have been less affected by those views, but I took them all in, wanting to please and do the "right" thing. Even when I was out to my family about my queer sexuality, before I told them about gender, the LGBTQ+ community was always the butt of a joke, and I was humourless for not laughing too. Though I'm sure it wasn't the intention of those surrounding me, my queerness and my transness had been forced into being uncomfortable secrets. The closet was where I was supposed to take them, and when I refused to put them away in there, the trade-off was shame and isolation.

In the media and popular culture, we often hear that it is "inappropriate" for trans people to exist around children. It's exactly the same thing that many LGB people in the UK heard until recently; Section 28 was abolished in 2003, same-sex marriage was granted – in England and Wales – in 2013 and an eventual shift has come about in society's views towards sexuality. Of course, the fight for acceptance and respect towards the LGB part of the community is not over, but I feel it is fair to say that the attitudes towards trans, non-binary and gender non-conforming people are a generation or two behind.

Recent protests outside schools in Birmingham are alarming to me because they arose from children simply being read a book which included a character who had two mummies.

What on earth might reactions be to children having a trans, queer teacher? My identity is not fictional – I am a living, breathing person – and it is not harmful either. My children will have two non-binary parents, and our family will be just as valid as anyone else's. The children in my future classes will have a trans teacher, but will be receiving just as good an education as any class with a cisgender teacher. The thought of doing all the things a teacher needs to do, alongside fearing that protests will erupt about my right to exist and teach as who I am, intimidates me sometimes.

During my short time in the education world, I have heard the following: my identity is unprofessional; parents won't like their children "being told lies about gender"; I'm confusing young girls into thinking they have to be men; people like me are grooming young people; I'm putting dangerous and confusing ideas into children's heads; children in primary school are too young to think about gender; I'm harming gay and lesbian children; I'm wrongly convincing children that being trans is "normal"; I'm pushing an agenda and I and other trans people are perverts. If this all sounds familiar, that's because it is: most of these things were (and are) said about LGB teachers too. But there's an added layer for trans teachers.

In my experience, a majority of the homophobic or transphobic people I've met look upon someone being gay as preferable to being trans. Like it's bad, but tolerably so, compared to the worst option. I think that comes from greater exposure to the concept that "love is love" and the fact that sexuality is about who you fancy, but gender identity is how you think about yourself. It tends to be that those who accept homosexuality but not transgender people do so because the idea that you can examine and unpick your received gender is too threatening to think about. I think we're all negatively affected by an enforced gender binary, meaning the existence of trans people touches a raw nerve for many. But it doesn't really make it any easier knowing that this is where the violence towards us stems from. A part of that vehement opposition to our existence is the wealth of anti-trans rhetoric in the media. The internet has become a minefield of disturbing anti-trans propaganda masquerading as support aimed at parents and schools. Maybe it's stupid to wade straight into that, but I don't know how else it's going to change, unless people have a human being to contrast that trans monster they've read about. Of course, the LGB community have faced this for themselves. I look to them and their narrative over time in the hope that the same – albeit gradual – change will come for those of us existing in the TQ+ part of the acronym.

Sometimes I'm in school and I'll hear a male colleague talking about being a man or a female colleague describing herself as a "strong woman", or another mentioning her husband. No one bats an eyelid. As well they shouldn't. But if I mention my gender, I notice an intake of breath from adults around me. If someone refers to a male teacher as "she" (a slip of the tongue that happens occasionally; we are a female-heavy profession), it's obviously funny and corrected immediately. Yet when I gather the strength to correct someone that I'm not a "she", or that I probably shouldn't be included in the "hello ladies" greeting, I'm met with confusion, annoyance or profuse over-apology that goes on all day. I'm not saying mistakes aren't allowed, just that it's tiring not to be recognised as casually as everyone else. My gender is shrouded in secrecy that other people put on it, when really it's as interesting and boring as anyone else's. This reinforces the need for education to happen around gender. And this reinforces my desire to become an educator. The reality is that no one else will do that work for trans people.

Once, after I had given an assembly about what transgender and non-binary are, some children asked me what "intersex" meant as they had heard the term during Pride month. I went to explain, but was hurriedly silenced by the class teacher. He told me later that he "didn't want them to be confused". Another time, I was told that I was giving away "too much personal information" when I said to a student that they could call me "they" or "he" and didn't mind which they chose to use. This was after they asked me if I was a "he, she or it".

I'm not offended by questions from children. Why would I be as a teacher? That's when learning happens! Moreover, it provides an opportunity for modelling or explicitly teaching being respectful and provides children with an accurate picture of the world. Children I work with continually astonish me with their engagement with queerness – whether they find it hard to accommodate new information or it makes complete sense to them. I have never ended a discussion with a child about queerness on an uncomfortable note. Usually, we chat about a question they have, and we listen to each other's experiences. I am always clear that if we have different opinions, that's totally fine! As long as we respect each other, we don't have to feel the same. I have no interest in persuading other people to identify how I do (especially children, who are busy figuring out how to be a person at all); I only want to be my whole self, showing others that they can be themselves too.

I should say that I feel very lucky about the number of people I've worked with who have been brilliant about accepting me, even if it was challenging to model inclusion of something unfamiliar at first. I've worked in schools where, even if they've not had an openly trans member of staff before, they've taken it in their stride and had all the right intentions. However, I question whether I should feel "lucky" that most of my colleagues have treated me with the same respect they treat others, rather than simply expectant of this.

A major issue in education is that the majority of primary teachers are white, cisgender, middle-class women, and a huge amount of children are not and will never be a part of those groups. There is nothing wrong with this, but the world that children are a part of contains many more kinds of people than that. I strongly feel that children need to see both reflections of themselves in those who guide them and the kinds of people they are not so familiar with, so they know that the world exists beyond their "bubble". This comes from my own experiences as a child and from observing what is happening around me in schools. I don't seek to just be a role model for the relatively small number of children who will question their gender, but to show every pupil that we are all different from each other, and that is the most ordinary thing that we all share. And we have so much in common beyond the borders of identity.

In the bigger picture, I believe all workplaces should actively try to employ staff from a diverse range of backgrounds and cultures that reflects the real world. It has been proven that diversity in thinking and experience results in the most creative and high-quality work, as Matthew Syed's 2019 book *Rebel Ideas*[1] attests to. Positive discrimination is likely not the best long-term strategy, but we have to acknowledge that workplaces the world over – including in education – have an imbalance that needs to be redressed. But in terms of what I can do right now as an individual, being openly myself is the most powerful tool I have.

By silencing marginalised identities, you do not stop them from existing. Whether or not you agree that I am who I am does not change the fact that I am here, being me, as normal and different as everybody else. Children are already a part of a world where gender theory and reality are becoming more expansive. We have a responsibility to our young people to help them engage with and understand the world and themselves, not bury our heads in the sand and teach about the least challenging, most black-and-white version of life. In my mind, that is not setting children up to succeed or teaching them to dream big. I work in the early years and have had complex, honest and appropriate discussions with three- to seven-year-olds that they raise and are ready for. Almost all teenagers I meet know someone who identifies as trans or non-binary, and record numbers of young people are now identifying as "not straight" in some way. It's up to us to teach respect for LGBTQ+ identities with the same gravity we give to race, cis-normative gender and religion.

Besides, we all contain multitudes. You know about my gender, but did you also know I am Jewish, a fiancé, a dog-dad, a bit of a grandpa who's terrible with computers, an art enthusiast, a nature lover and a huge Bowie nerd? I have facets of my identity that give me immense privilege – for instance, I am white and able-bodied – aspects of who I am that people use to discriminate against me – for example, my faith/heritage, sexuality and gender identity – and parts of me that aren't as simple to make snap judgements on – having an "invisible disibility" (dyspraxia) – and the socio-economic grey area I grew up in. All people – children included – are complex, and I have no doubt that there is space in our education system to think in an intersectional way about identity. It's an opportunity for everyone to be happier, more seen, more understanding.

I tiptoe the line between being strong and vocal, and I'm fearing that an explosion is just around the corner. I ended up resigning from one job I had in a school because they over-scrutinised every interaction I had with pupils (such as asking how their day had been), believing that I was encouraging them to be trans. I felt both threatened and feared when I was hauled in for "reviews" that went over my line manager's head. Even though I know I did nothing wrong, the shame stuck with me. But I cannot shake the feeling that it is so important to be visible. Being trans, non-binary and working in education now feels a bit like being at the front of a tidal wave.

I took a year out of my studies to work in a primary school last year, and when I left to return to university, children throughout the years had made me a card. In almost all of their colourful drawings and messages, they alluded to pride, being yourself and queerness. I lost count of the numbers of rainbows drawn, and some of the most special things they had written were "thank you for boosting my confidence and letting me be myself", "keep on spreading the pride message!", "pride matters" and "love for everyone". Whilst I suppose I don't dress like most of my colleagues and am visibly a bit "different", I hadn't necessarily spoken to many children about queerness, as I was employed to work very closely with just two. But educators cannot underestimate the impact they have on a whole school full of young lives. It seemed that all the small things I did to make sure I was myself at work had communicated a message of acceptance. I didn't expect Years 3 and 4 to remember what I had said to them in one assembly, months ago, about gender identity. But they did. I didn't expect a few children who had learned about my pronouns to correct others or use them confidently. But they did. I didn't expect to be far more supported and celebrated by a bunch of 7- to 11-year-olds than I have ever felt by adults. But I did. Children do not underestimate us as positive role models, and in turn, we should not underestimate them as sensitive, welcoming and kind human beings with a need to see honesty in those they look to for guidance.

## Big gay notes from the editor

*"In my experience, a majority of the homophobic or transphobic people I've met look upon someone being gay as preferable to being trans"*. This is the first time this book tackles the idea of levels of privilege where, as a trans person, Kip is also white and able-bodied but does not experience discrimination for that. It can be argued that the perceived battle in the media, currently, is for trans rights more than LGB. Certainly some of the language in the tabloid press around trans issues is similar in toxicity to some of the language around gay people and AIDS in the 1980s.

Later chapters will look more at intersectionality: the idea that a person is not merely gay or white or male or trans, but can be all of these and more. Kip describes themselves as "Jewish, a fiancé, a dog dad, terrible with computers, a nature lover and a huge Bowie nerd". Why are so many of these labels, which help build positive relationships with young people and their interests, considered "appropriate" when trans is not? A key thought from this chapter is where Kip states that different things were expected of them when they were perceived as a girl compared to their friends who were boys. We have to be conscious as teachers to not have different expectations dependent on gender identity, and we need to promote the same equality of opportunity for LGBT+ young people.2 Children look to us to be positive role models as kind, honest and sensitive human beings just like we would want to promote the same qualities in them.

## Notes

1 Matthew Syed (2020) *Rebel Ideas: The Power of Diverse Thinking*.
2 Further recommended reading on this topic would be Matt Pinkett and Mark Roberts (2019) *Boys Don't Try: Rethinking Masculinity in Schools*.

# 6 Permission

*Chris Mattley*

*Chris Mattley is 36 years old and currently teaches at William Farr CofE School near Lincoln. Chris read BA Geography at Jesus College, Oxford University, before completing his Postgraduate Certificate In Education (PGCE) at St Anne's College, Oxford University. He currently holds the position of Head of Year and won a Silver Award in the Pearson National Teaching Awards in 2015. He once owned a toy lawnmower.*

Teaching is definitely an emotional rollercoaster. Dealing with so many different variables all pulling against one another on a daily basis requires a lot of resilience. The teacher, amongst all the egos and challenges, is meant to be professional and remain calm in the face of whatever happens in the classroom. Add into this mix the prospect of telling staff and children that you are gay and you can see why so many people choose to this day to stay in the education closet at the back of their classrooms.

I grew up in the era of Section 28. Section 28 was a piece of legislation that existed in the UK and came into effect in May 1988. It told local authorities that they should not promote homosexuality or say that two men or two women could be a family. I never knew it existed. I didn't know what it was. But Section 28 shaped my life. My entire development as a young man was devoid of a supportive environment where someone who I respected and trusted could give me information about how I was feeling so that I could make sense of the chaos in my head. Instead, I only had one source when it came to anything that was gay or lesbian, gay, bisexual and trans (LGBT), the media and in particularly printed newspapers. Through these outlets I was told that the way I felt was abhorrent and unnatural, I was told that I would get AIDS and die alone and I was told that I was unwanted and that my existence was not welcome in society. For a scared young teenager, the result was catastrophic. I hid. I denied my own existence out of one primal need – survival.

Section 28 was finally repealed in 2003, but this meant I spent my entire education feeling odd, different and hating who I was. The level of shame I felt cannot be quantified, and more importantly, shame is something that sticks around.

The Section 28 stench still hangs over education. I remember training to become a teacher in 2006. The issue of being LGBT was brought up during the entire process of a PGCE once. Don't. Don't mention it, don't discuss it and certainly do not disclose your sexual orientation to anyone. The logic was that it was not professional and would put your entire career at risk. Being openly gay in a school would leave you vulnerable to attack and ridicule and undermine your status as a teacher. Desperate to be the best teacher I could be, the bolt on my closet stayed firmly shut.

I have been teaching for 13 years in the same school that I completed my Newly Qualified Teacher placement. It is a Church of England school, a fact which has added complications with regard to the issue of being LGBT. As a place of work it is a supportive environment, with colleagues that have inspired me to be the best practitioner I could, so it is no wonder I've never left. For the first seven years of my time at school, I lied. I hid in plain sight, making up potential heterosexual dates to even my closest of friends. I revelled in the safety provided when students assumed I was dating a female colleague. But the shame that I felt when I was younger never went away. For now while I had come to terms with my sexuality, the shame I now felt was one of guilt and deception. Lying to all around me made me feel like a fraud. So I tried to effect change in subtle ways. When the task came to create the Personal, Social and Health Education (PSHE) curriculum, the seemingly "sensitive" issue of teaching about homosexuality and homophobia came up. More experienced staff shied away, some even questioned why they should be teaching it at all, so I volunteered to write the lessons that would be delivered to the school. Using resources from Stonewall, I created a small pocket of change. But I was still hiding my authentic self. The true me.

The catalyst for change came when my tutor group entered Year 12. A new student, fresh from the USA, asked if the school has a Gay Straight Alliance (GSA). I had no idea what this was and had to ask; they explained that it was a GSA. Some gay man I was! But then, why would I have known? My education was devoid of the word gay. It was a slur, a term of hatred and derision. I explained that the school had openly gay students and a strong stance against homophobic bullying, and so there was no real need for one. But the question had planted a seed which didn't go away. The school had other support groups, a Christian Union; why couldn't it have an LGBT space? The student who asked about the GSA was struggling to find their place and this would benefit them immensely. Tentatively I asked more senior colleagues about the possibility. Initially, they gave the same response I had given, as a tolerant school that promoted equality for all, we have never had the need for one. But now a need had arisen. With some careful diplomacy and support from a senior member of staff, a Wednesday lunchtime club appeared on the school's daily bulletin. The first meeting was just myself and the student in my form. Humble beginnings.

But I had put my head above the parapet. Rumours abound in the staffroom. I was running the "gay" club in a Church of England school. The whispers grew louder. "Is he gay too?" But still I hid. I was haunted by the advice given during my PGCE, and coming out at school was career suicide. I had worked hard to establish myself as a teacher within the school. I'd built a reputation as a hard worker, students enjoyed the lessons I made, I turned my books in marked and on time. On reflection I think I'd done this, as so many aspects of my life, as cover. If I could be good, if I could please, if I could give no one reason to attack me, maybe they wouldn't attack me because I was gay. For two more years I said nothing. The lesbian, gay, bisexual, trans and others (LGBT+) Space we had created went from strength to strength. Assemblies led by myself and students discussed key LGBT figures, gender and sexuality and tackled hate and homophobia, biphobia and transphobia. A feeling of pride had begun to form where there had only been shame and fear. I was in a stable relationship outside of school and finally reached a place where I felt I could be brave, braver than I'd ever been, in a place that for me was the one place you had to be a version of yourself.

So nine years into my teaching career I booked an appointment with the headteacher. I had to give a reason for the appointment. Personal I thought. This was personal right? I remember waiting outside his office on the chairs where students wait after an exclusion. Palms sweaty and my foot tapping. On that day, I asked permission to come out in school. Reflecting back on it now I recoil at that statement. Permission. My headteacher did the exact same thing. "Why are you asking for my permission?" he asked. I hadn't expected this response. I took a deep breath and explained my logic. I needed to ask permission because I did not want the school to get into trouble. As a Church of England school I did not want to cause problems with parents, the local diocese and bring unnecessary attention to the school. "OK, so why now?" he calmly asked. I took another breath and took him through my journey at the school; he had been one of the senior members of staff who had employed me fresh from PGCE training. I explained how I'd worked hard to establish myself as a good teacher and build a reputation, and that I was in a position to make a difference. "But why now?" came the response. Here was the moment when the shame and guilt bubbled to the surface. I told him how I'd been advised to hide that aspect of my life, and as a result professionally I'd lived a lie, conveniently hiding in plain sight. The guilt of lying to students who had unreservedly placed their trust and confidence in me as a role model had become too much to bear. I was a hypocrite. If by being open made one student change their mind about LGBT people, allowed one student to see a different perspective from what may be a very homophobic home or helped one student feel less alone, then it would all be worth it. I wanted for just one student to have what I never had, a visible role model that was confident and could inspire me to not feel like I was unwelcome in the world. "That's all I needed to hear", he replied. We talked for a good hour about experiences of being LGBT in a society that has come so far, and he told me that I had never needed to seek his permission, but that he had respected the care and humility I had shown to the school by even asking him.

So now I was out, to the headteacher at least. What was next? The LGBT+ Space had been around for three years and was prominent feature in our Church of England school. Students who identified as LGBT+ or who were just allies came to our weekly lunchtime meeting. But I was still a whisper in the staffroom and still wearing a mask to the student community. At this stage, I had been Head of Year for two years. This meant I had to give a weekly assembly. What is more visible than an assembly? A theme of an upcoming assembly was about "Personal Growth", and I decided to use some pictures to create a timeline of moments from childhood to now to show that reflection and taking stock was just as important as striving onwards, head down, powering through to the next achievement. The moment was all of five seconds. In amongst pictures of my first toy lawnmower, my first computer console and acne riddled photobooth poses with friends, I said it. "And it was about here that I realised I was gay". I carried on. Didn't stop. The rest of the assembly carried on. It wasn't mentioned again. I'd said it, it was out. Walking back to my first class of the day, I followed a group of students in my year group. "I knew it…I told you!" one student remarked. "You didn't believe me but I knew". I caught up and asked what it was that he knew, and the group scuttled onwards and I chuckled to myself. I was lighter than air. Why wouldn't I be? The weight of all my professional guilt and shame had just been left in the Main Hall.

The LGBT+ Space and School are now nationally recognised for the support we give to LGBT+ students and their parents. We have spoken at Stonewall's Education for All conference; the students have provided teacher training for staff and also spoken to National Health Service (NHS) professionals at local countywide conferences for four consecutive years. The school has gender neutral toilets and has supported students transitioning and their parents. Students choose to trust me with their most precious truths, and I cannot explain how incredible that feeling is. Whether it is a student who hangs around at the end of a Geography lesson about coastal erosion to tell me that they are pansexual and they just wanted me to know, or the successful football captain in my year group that told me three years ago that he was gay and he wanted me to know because of my assembly, the rewards of being a visible LGBT teacher reach far and wide. Students have told me that just knowing that the LGBT+ Space exists in school is enough for them, they might not be as far on their journey as I am, but knowing that it is there fills them with hope. Trans students have said that while their parents have rejected their gender identity, that being called the right name and the right pronouns at school has saved their lives.

I'm reminded of something I heard Sir Ian McKellen say to a group of students. He said that when you are LGBT, you don't come out once. You come out every day. You make a choice to tell the world about you, and that is every person you meet. When you sit in a taxi or in the barber's chair and someone asks if you are doing anything nice with your girlfriend, you have to decide whether to correct them or not. Sometimes you will, sometimes you choose not to. This is not the place for a discussion about the etiquette and label of being openly gay and far more eloquent people have said much better words than I will, but his words have stayed with me to this day. I used to tell myself and others that my sexuality was as important to me as my little finger nail. It was a small part of me. It didn't define me. It was something that I happened to be. I didn't lead with it or shout it from the roof tops. There were other aspects of my personality and character that were far more important and on one level that sentiment remains true. However, in my role as an educator, the power of being a visible gay man has never been more important. While I might not wave a giant flag every day and it does not dominate every conversation I have, I put a rainbow pin badge on my suit and I represent. For young LGBT+ students and those students who are not, my job, every day, is to say unequivocally that it is ok to be gay.

## Big gay notes from the editor

*"Why are you asking for my permission?" the headteacher asked. It is not uncommon in my experience for colleagues to "ask" before they can come out, and this headteacher's response was particularly refreshing. Many "out" LGBT+ teachers have approached their headteachers to check the mood in the room. Will they be supportive? Can they be counted on to defend their staff in the event of any potential backlash? Similar questions to these go through almost every LGBT+ person's mind before coming out. It could be considered polite and professional practice to consult the headteacher first, and their reaction may be the difference between whether you choose to stay at that school or whether you choose to move on to somewhere else.*

*In this chapter, Chris Mattley touches on the ingrained culture of fear – fear of AIDS, fear of dying alone, fear of backlash – that permeates the psyche of so many LGBT+ people and he, like me, was told during his training that coming out would be career suicide. So he stayed in the closet in order to be the best teacher he could be. I too spent the first few years building up a reputation as a reliable teacher, a teacher who is respected by students who learn a lot in my lessons. This is the most important thing in teaching, of course, and it can offer more "leverage" with the leadership team if done well. However, since being "out", I have also found the sense of fulfilment in my role to be much stronger. I am able to connect with students on a more human level, and this benefits them as young people trying to find their niche in the world.*

*Research shows[1] that ability to be our authentic and true selves at work is an enormous motivating factor and the power of this cannot be underestimated – particularly during a recruitment and retention crisis in the profession. It is also equally valid that leaders should expect authenticity from their employees. Some of the quick wins are already in place at Chris's school – the LGBT+ Space and assemblies about "personal growth" for example – but, overall, Chris argues that in our roles as educators, the power of being a visible LGBT+ person has never been more important.*

## Note

1 Vanessa Buote (2019) *Why You Should Bring Your Authentic Self to Work* in Harvard Business Review: https://hbrascend.org/topics/why-you-should-bring-your-authentic-self-to-work/

# 7 A story in two halves

*Catherine Halliwell and Cerian Craske*

*Catherine Halliwell is a proudly 'out' teacher. He is currently Head of Science at Nonsuch High School for Girls after teaching in London schools for 18 years. In addition to advocating for the lesbian, gay, bisexual, trans and others (LGBT+) community in the school, across the Trust, borough and beyond, she is a school Mental Health Champion. Cerian Craske is currently a second year English student at Cambridge and she was part of the group who founded the Nonsuch LGBT+ Society. This chapter tells the same story from two different perspectives: that of an 'out' teacher and that of a student whose life was changed as a result.*

## Being an 'out' teacher

This story begins with a single email at school:

> Dear Ms Halliwell. We'd like to set up an LGBT+ society in school. Can you help please?

Of course, my first joke was 'hmmm, why me darling?!'

This was 2015, not 1985, when I was at school. Although I grew up in the era of Section 28, when the Tory Party's disdain distinctly flavoured my childhood in the North of England, I had long ago learnt I was happier *out* rather than *in* the closet. This journey had been difficult and I knew coming out was a lifelong commitment. I did not realise I was not yet an out teacher in school.

I was in my forties and I had been in a long-term relationship for seven years. I had been *out* to staff at my first school and now at my second. I regularly talked about my girlfriend, and all her escapades as she travelled with work, often leaving home for weeks at a time. Occasionally I would mention 'my partner' in front of students.

However, receiving this short email changed my life – my perspective, my self-respect and allowed a slow trickle of events, opportunities and emotions to cascade into a tsunami of activism quietly advocating for the umbrella of queer folk in school – becoming an 'out' teacher.

My initial meeting with the students was blessed by a supportive Pastoral senior leadership team (SLT) member. We quickly defined the simple aims of the group – to provide a safe space for students to meet and support each other in school. However, we soon became motivated to reach beyond ourselves and into the wider school during the following months.

The next academic year I was funded to attend a Stonewall 'Train the Trainer' Continuing Professional Development (CPD) session, and I worked with the students to update our

Personal, Social and Health Education (PSHE) resources to be LGBT+ inclusive. The atmosphere of the society built trust and community, as we all developed our confidence.

As our initial Year 10 students entered the sixth form we launched our first LBGT+ History Month with our inaugural Big Gay Bake Sale, a treasured 15-minute smash and grab session in the school hall, raising 250 pounds for Stonewall. All that remained were crumbs, smiles from deep inside our gay hearts and many thanks to the hundreds of students and staff that descended.

We packaged our History Month with registration activities, quizzes and role model posters across the school – that are still in place three years later – and a timely reminder of our bullying policy, including bi-, homo- and transphobic bullying.

Over time our self-assurance grew – we now have a Pride Week each July, which coincides with Sports Day (lots of opportunities for flags), Open Evening (we love a good conversation with prospective parents) and this year the school birthday (85 years young) when we co-ordinated with the history department to produce a school-wide activity linking *Riots and Rights* to demonstrate that civil disobedience and rights are the foundation of our society – remembering the 50 year anniversary of Stonewall.

However, it was in July 2018 during our first Pride Week that I truly understood what being an out teacher meant. Local LGBT+ activist and senior citizen Ray Harvey-Amer came into school to discuss the changes to LGBT+ rights he had witnessed during his lifetime and the issues outstanding. He was genuinely moved to tears on entering the school foyer to see the large rainbow and trans flags flying proudly. His near disbelief at the contrast with his own school life was palpable.

In the following 15-minute assembly, the society shared their experiences at Pride and those of other students and staff. When my turn came to speak, I looked out to see Ray, all the students and staff. I could barely utter a word, realising the three generations of LGBT+ community around me and the weight of that responsibility. As I turned and shared my first Pride photograph, I took a deep breath and held my head up high, to rise above my fears to address the hall. I really was proud. I was certainly now an 'out' teacher.

I am fortunate that the journey of LGBT+ support continues in my school, and together we welcome difficult discussions with an understanding of associated mental health issues. Our LGBT+ allies are all across the school – from rainbow lanyard wearing staff to students delivering ally PSHE activities.

I am still learning what an "out" leader looks like, does, feels and shares. I am forever grateful to the brave students who initially stood up and asked for help. Hopefully my out life demonstrates the difference our small actions and attitudes can make for others. I continue to lead in school across the borough and have taken part in national events, especially incorporating mental health discussions.

I am indebted to my school for supporting all the LGBT+ students and staff to be safe as their authentic selves. Thank you to all the awesome allies and the next out generation. Visibility really does matter.

My final words come from a founding member of the LGBT+ society: 'it was so important to me having a LGBT+ figure who I could look up to and later work with … I'm still getting involved with LGBT+ at university.'

## Having an 'out' teacher

When we first sent off the email to Ms Halliwell which would lead to the formation of the LGBT+ society, there was one main concern on our minds – did we guess wrong? We didn't want to have wrongly assumed that a teacher was gay (even though we'd said nothing of the sort in the email, just asked for help). Despite this, all of us – young, newly out at school as LGBT+ and trying to find our place in the world – had known from the start that Ms Halliwell would be the best person to turn to. As it turned out, we were right, and that email was the start of something which would permanently change my experience of the school.

LGBT+ society started small. We took over one of the school IT rooms once a week, brought Skittles and Smarties and tried to educate people about our experiences and provide a safe space for other LGBT+ students. It had never been hard for people to tell that I was gay – to this day, the only family members I've 'officially' come out to are my parents, the rest guessed long before I had to tell them – but at that point I was still nervous, still trying to figure out what my identity actually meant for the rest of my life. LGBT+ narratives did, and still do, overwhelmingly focus on teenagers and on the process of coming out itself, so once I felt like I'd completed that particular chapter, I had no idea what I was supposed to do next. No one teaches you how to exist as a gay person (not that anyone teaches you how to exist in general, I suppose), and I found it hard to project what my life would look like, a struggle which I'm sure is familiar to other LGBT+ people. Having a visibly LGBT+ teacher combatted this, as for the first time there was someone older than me who wasn't just another student, who had a life and friends and a job, and I found it a little less hard to visualise myself as a gay adult.

The society changed over the years. The initial committee of us who set it up was made up of three couples, and since we were all 15, this dissolved fairly quickly, leaving other people to take the reins. I no longer needed the group in quite the same way over the next year or two, but I found myself going back and speaking to the younger students, trying to show them the same potential for the future that I'd felt. One of the greatest moments was our Big Gay Bake Sale, in which we filled the school hall with rainbows and sugar and blasted gay anthems over the sound system, and sold out of cakes within minutes. Admittedly, it's easier to get people to support you if you give them cake, but it still felt pretty good to know that everyone knew we were gay and proud and was happy to give us their support.

After I left school, I came back in to help out with Pride Week, and to stand up in front of teachers I'd known for years and students I'd never met was such an incredibly empowering experience which I never would have had if Ms Halliwell hadn't responded favourably to that email years ago. I also brought in Ray Harvey-Amer, local LGBT+ activist and one of my family friends, who was astonished at the sheer amount of LGBT+ visibility in the school – I didn't know how to respond to this, because I was surprised as well, as even in the short time I'd been at school attitudes had changed so much.

I'm a second year at university now – I've been as involved as possible in the LGBT+ community, with LGBT+ open mic nights and pride events forming a significant part of my timetable. I'll admit that when I went back to school recently to run a workshop, running into Ms Halliwell and letting her know that I'm still 'living my best gay life' felt great. I've definitely grown up a long way from the nervous 15-year-old who sent off that email, and it's been amazing to see how the school has changed even in the short time since I left, with far more LGBT+ visibility than my younger self could ever have dreamed of.

## Big gay notes from the editor

*'Dear Ms Halliwell. We'd like to set up an LGBT+ society in school. Can you help please?' These words surmise perfectly how powerful a visible LGBT+ role model can be and why we need them in all schools. It is a request for help from a student reaching out to somebody they look up to. Sadly, not all students are in a position to openly ask for help so we need to be the ones to offer it.*

*Catherine writes how she is forever grateful to the brave students who initially stood up and asked for help, and what is so wonderful about this chapter is how Cerian Craske – the former student who is now a very confident young gay person – also shares her version of events. This clearly demonstrates their positive relationship that has been impactful over time, and I couldn't help but be moved by it. I'm sure many of you will be too. This story in two halves exemplifies that – as I wrote in my opening chapter – these are real human experiences shared by real people.*

*As teachers and leaders, LGBT+ people and allies, we have to make it our mission to anticipate those questions that some students may not have the confidence to ask. We have to consider what questions we would have asked at school and how we would have made our experiences more positive if we had the choice. There is no definitive description of what an 'out' leader is, but it means being the role models we needed when we were at school. Later in this book, acclaimed writer Hadley Stewart also recounts his experiences of being taught English by an 'out' teacher at school.*

# 8 Intersections of identity
## Being an 'out' Jewish bisexual teacher

*Allison Zionts*

*Allison Zionts is a secondary school teacher in a girls' school in South London and a PhD student at Goldsmiths, University of London, where she is studying inclusion policies to support lesbian, gay, bisexual, transgender, queer and others (LGBTQ+) students in single-sex schools. She is originally from Pittsburgh, Pennsylvania; is a trustee of KeshetUK (the Jewish LGBT+ charity) and a staff governor for her school. In her spare time, Allison runs her school's local LGBTQ+ Pride and Rainbow Clubs, completed the CTeach programme at the Chartered College of Teaching and, like so many other teachers, takes long naps.*

My decision to 'come out' as a bisexual woman growing up was never a torturous one for me. With thanks to the community I had been raised in, which included a progressive Jewish upbringing and a family background in musical theatre, I was surrounded by members of the LGBTQ+ community from a young age in my hometowns of Pittsburgh and Montreal. This does not mean, however, that my coming out was a straightforward process; I do not remember the first person I came out to, nor when exactly it happened. I considered myself to be 'out' of the closet, even if I had not disclosed my attraction orientation to everyone, because I never felt the need to hide who I was. I was, in that way, exceptionally lucky. Upon reflection, my sexual identity was one that I was more comfortable sharing with people as I got older, as I was concerned that my Jewish identity would prove to be problematic in secular and queer circles.

I moved to London in 2010 to begin my teaching career and was hired as a Health and Social Care teacher at an all-girls school in Croydon. I had been warned that this school was difficult, and that the students were 'rougher' than average. I stayed in that school for five years, which helped to develop my identity as a teacher while also coming to terms with being an 'outsider' and having to deal with the new lingo of British schools. Being an obvious outsider, I was nervous and unsure about how to go about forging my identity as a Jewish bisexual woman in a space where I had felt so uncomfortable every time I had a student question my accent or word choice.

I tested the waters of sharing my identity midway through my first year in the school, and I told them that I was Jewish. For the first time in my life, I was greeted with animosity rather than curiosity. Staff told me that I should not have divulged that part of my identity to the students, because it would just make me look different. Students recounted stories and stereotypes they had heard about Jews and asked me to prove they were not true – were all Jews really rich? Are they really in charge of all the politics? Did they go to separate schools because they thought they were better than their non-Jewish counterparts? While I was shocked that in the twenty-first century, these rumours and ideas were still prevalent, I was more confused that neither my colleagues nor their parents seemed to stand up for me when students raised these rather confronting points. Nevertheless, I persisted in sharing my Jewish identity with my students when the topic arose, and after two years, I witnessed a shift in my students' understanding of how my own religious diversity was not a problem or a concern, but rather a facet of my identity, just like being Christian or Muslim was a facet in theirs. I began an interfaith forum in my classroom during the month of Ramadan, and the students from various religious backgrounds opened up about the importance of dialogue in order to learn more about the cultures.

The parents, however, were not as open and welcoming to having a Jewish teacher be with their children. Three parents asked for their children to be removed from my tutor group, as they were uncomfortable with how I may corrupt their children regarding faith. While the school leaders eventually sided with me and ensured the students remained in my tutor group without incident from the parents, I knew that this was not a school where I could be comfortable being my authentic self in the long-term. If school leaders were reticent to support a Jewish teacher who was facing anti-Semitic comments from their students and teachers, how would they support LGBTQ+ staff?

I had already seen that students who were knew that they were queer did not feel comfortable sharing this publically within the school. The school leaders had rejected their requests for a Pride celebration or assembly, and the mere perception that a student may be part of the LGBTQ+ community opened them up to ridicule and bullying from their peers. For the first time in my life, I felt uncomfortable in terms of my sexual identity. I was worried about other teachers finding out about who I was, and the horror stories that I had read about – teachers being ridiculed in staff rooms or bullied by school leaders until they left the school – had shocked me, particularly as I could see that happening in this school.

In 2014, I applied to teach in a school that should have been, by all intents and purposes, quite similar to my first school: they were both South London all-girl schools with similar demographics in terms of ethnicity, social class and students with special educational needs. My tour around the school was a young Muslim girl, proudly wearing a school pin to fasten her hijab. As I often ask students when visiting schools, I inquired as to what was the best part of the year so far. This student excitedly told me about a recent school visit by Sir Ian McKellen as part of the Stonewall Role Models programme. Speaking to the entire school population, Sir McKellen had delivered an impassioned speech regarding the importance of inclusion and developing a diverse and celebratory school community. I knew from this moment that this was a school I wanted to be a part of.

In my interview, I made it clear that this school appealed to me because of its commitment to multiculturalism and diversity within its staff and student population. I specifically had named the school's LGBTQ+ programmes as the reason why the school was my top choice for the next move in my career. Upon joining the school, I quickly opened up to the staff and students that I was Jewish and was met with curiosity rather than stereotypes. Similar to my first school, the vast majority of the staff and students had never met a Jewish person before, but their attitudes towards someone different allowed me to be proud of my identity, rather than constantly feeling the need to defend it. I have been asked to check over the assembles for Holocaust Memorial Day each year, not in a way that suggested tokenism, but rather to ensure the message to the school is consistent with the current beliefs and understanding of the Holocaust from someone with more insider knowledge than the average teacher.

Part way through my first year at the school, I founded the Rainbow Club, a space for students to discuss LGBTQ+ issues within the school and wider community. It was in this space that I told my students that I was a part of the LGBTQ+ community, and while revealing my Jewish identity had been met with questions, the students took this disclosure as a normal occurrence. While at the time, as well as currently at the time of writing, I am the only out LGBTQ+ member of staff in my school, the students are not shielded from positive role models and examples of LGBTQ+ people and families throughout their curricula. Emerging from the Rainbow Club, the school had asked me to run workshops on being an LGBTQ+ advocate and activist as a young person and trans-inclusive feminism for our annual 'International Women's Day' and 'International Day of the Girl' conferences.

In October 2017, at the plenary session following our International Day of the Girl conference, one student announced that my workshop had given him the courage to come out publicly as a trans male student. While I had expected this to shock the school – a school that had been, for more than a century, proud of its all-girls status – the disclosure was met with thunderous applause. The school quickly adapted to using masculine pronouns for this student and began to make the adjustments necessary for having male students in the girls' school. While it is still a process, this boy's bravery demonstrated the compassion and support provided by my school, that inclusion was a core tenant of our beliefs. In the three years since, other students have come out and have looked up to this boy as a role model for someone who was comfortable being himself in a space where that may not have otherwise been welcome.

After that incident, the Rainbow Club grew so large it was divided into four Clubs – one for each of the Key Stages in the school and one for transgender and gender non-conforming students. From the beginning, they knew that this space was theirs. We meet in my classroom, which is decorated with a range of Pride flags representing different identities, and they lead the conversations about any LGBTQ+ topics they feel important at the time – sometimes Drag Race and pop culture, but oftentimes this is a space for them to reflect on instances of LGBTQ+ inclusion in the curriculum and school life. At Sports Days, the students drape flags around themselves as cloaks and have said that they feel 'invincible' and like Super Heroes – both showing students who aren't yet out that it's okay, while pre-empting any ridicule from potential bullies. The annual assembly on LGBTQ+ pride turned into three weeks of assemblies, ranging from LGBTQ+ history to Pride, and including a week on how people from different ethnic and religious communities have expressed their LGBTQ+ pride.

The students in Rainbow Club – who are both members of the LGBTQ+ community and allies – have given me strength to be more publicly out as a Jewish bisexual woman. This isn't to say that I discuss it every day with each of my classes – in fact, my identity rarely comes up! But I have been able to be authentically me and model for them what it means to be an adult who is comfortable with her identity. It is my hope not only that they have the strength to be comfortable with who they are now, but that they will continue to be beacons for their peers and the next generation.

## Big gay notes from the editor

*Returning to the topic of intersectionality, it is important to acknowledge that there is no one 'label' that fits all. Allison is bisexual and she is also Jewish. This brings its own distinct sense of community as well as its own set of challenges. Already feeling like an outsider, it was actually disclosing her identity as Jewish that provoked the strongest reaction from colleagues in her first school. It 'made her look different.' With this revelation to students came an opportunity to challenge stereotypes about Jewish people. Is it not our job as teachers to encourage critical independent thought and to promote inclusion? It can be incredibly exhausting to be the only individual member of staff standing up for these values for the students in our schools. We need our allies at all levels. In Allison's case, the negative response to revealing part of her identity led to her questioning what else she could ever reveal and whether she was in the right school. In turn, school leaders should question whether they have enabled a toxic culture like this in their own schools – inadvertently or otherwise – and how this might impact on retaining effective and motivated teachers. Ultimately she changed schools to find a better sense of belonging elsewhere.*

*In contrast, her experience in her next school was markedly different. There is a burning injustice that results in some students having a less inclusive and welcoming experience at school than others simply because of which school they attend. By living her authentic true self, Allison gave one student the courage come out as trans. The school's overwhelmingly positive response to this, including simple steps such as adapting the promouns used to refer to this person, will have made a huge difference to that child and – statistically – may have saved a life.*

# 9 You can't win on culture alone, but you sure can lose on it

*James Bennett*

*James Bennett is an English teacher at Ark Academy in Wembley. Prior to that he led a department and set up a range of equality and diversity initiatives in Islington schools. He takes part in Teach First's lesbian, gay, bisexual, trans and others (LGBT+) network and has written for the TES, The Guardian and other publications about his experiences.*

> It's important for teachers to be LGBTQ+ role models and allies because it shows us that there are people like us, we LGBTQ+ students don't feel alone and have supportive teachers to fall back on.
>
> Anonymous – Age 15

Scribbled in my teacher planner I have a constant reminder of my favourite mantra from our principal, 'you can't win on culture alone, but you sure can lose on it'. The culture of a school is something tangible that you can feel; it emanates from the classrooms, the corridors and the playground. Of course, culture isn't enough to get every child to where they need to go, but if it isn't right, staff and students suffer.

When I was a teenager, no one in my school was openly gay and I suffered for it. I felt isolated and hid my true identity. Students said, 'that's so gay' without a moment's thought and without consequence. Apart from a lesson about STDs, I don't remember ever discussing LGBT+ topics. Outside of school things were not much better, it was the age of 'Little Britain' and 'Ugly Betty'. But I didn't want to be a fashion designer or a caricature, so finding my place was difficult.

Many years later, the opportunities and acceptance I found at university fuelled my decision to help improve a system that is simply not working for the majority of young people who identify as LGBT+. Studies show almost half of all LGBT pupils face bullying and 'frequently' hear homophobic, biphobic or transphobic slurs. More than two in five trans young people have tried to take their life.[1]

Even before entering the classroom, I knew I wanted to be the LGBT+ advocate and role model that I never had. Some of my colleagues have found this surprising – it was only in 2003 that the Labour government overturned Section 28. David Cameron admitted in 2009 that 'we got it wrong', but the situation for LGBT+ people is far from secure. Trans pupils fear that with new reform to the Gender Recognition Act (GRA), they won't be able to get the support they need until they are 18.

I knew that I had to be the change I wanted to see. I came to this realisation at an event for LGBT History Month, set up and run by the charity Schools Out. In a room surrounded by

LGBT activists, couples, families and academics, LGBT History Month founder Sue Sanders asked: 'Who in this room heard anything positive about LGBT people at school?' A deafening silence hit the room; no hands went up. I knew something had to change.

> I even remember a time where a teacher was putting us in our seating plan and the girl sitting next to me told the teacher that she wasn't comfortable sitting next to me because I am a lesbian.
>
> Anonymous – Age 14

Some colleagues were worried about the reactions I might get from students. I was prepared to fight my corner in the hope of being a good role model for young LGBT+ pupils, even if it meant dealing with verbal abuse.

At the most innocent level, now that I wear an engagement ring, I frequently get students and staff – who clearly didn't get the memo – ask about my wife and whether I have children. Next on the scale, there is the underlying uneasiness and uncertainty when encountering LGBT+ people. From staff members who question the need for celebrating or talking about LGBT+ History Month, to students who give you a strange look in the corridor, for some there is still the idea that talking about LGBT+ people is taboo. Then of course, there are more serious instances of discrimination. I am lucky that I have only been on a receiving end of homophobia from students a handful of times and have always had the support of fantastic school leaders.

Starting at my second school I encountered that conundrum that many LGBT+ people will be familiar with: when, being faces with coming 'out' again. I was very aware that the school community in this school was very different; there were few students who felt safe to comfortably 'out' and yet again, no staff who were out to students. Luckily for me, the first Friday morning Personal, Social and Health Education (PSHE) session with my Year 10 form was on homophobia. For many students, watching a Stonewall video and having a discussion is their only encounter with LGBT+ diversity in the curriculum. In my experience, children of all backgrounds respect teachers who can teach well, build relationships with them and be open and honest.

Just like Daniel Tomlinson-Gray and many others, before now I have encountered teachers and leaders who say, 'but why do you need to talk about your personal life?' The thing is, these are often the same teachers that have a photo of their wife on their desk and spend their assemblies talking about their family. The lingering spectre of Section 28 means that educators from the LGBT+ community are instantly accused of talking about the forbidden topic of sex. Yet, when heterosexual or cis colleagues talk about their family, of course that link isn't made.

In order for staff and students to feel safe, included and celebrated in schools, a policy against homophobia, biphobia and transphobia is not enough. In order to change hearts and minds school need to fulfil their requirements of the equalities act to eliminate discrimination, advance equality of opportunity and to foster good relations between groups of diverse people.

> Before this, I don't actually remember anything from school that made me feel included as a member of the community.
>
> Anonymous – Age 13

Many businesses and organisations recognise the need for support systems and networks for LGBT+ employees to feel accepted and valued and to perform at their best. Indeed, in education it appears things are starting to shift. Teach First, the education charity and teacher trainers, have recorded that nine per cent of their trainee teachers identify as LGBT+. I was lucky to be part of the training programme and take part in their LGBT+ network events and pride celebrations even before I had taught my first class. Teach First, which recruits around 1,400 teachers each year, said the increase is a sign of positive progress within schools and encourages all schools to create a welcoming and accepting environment for LGBT teachers.

In order to get the best from our pupils and our educators, we need to foster the same approaches as other workplaces and public institutions. The majority of schools have systems in place to take homophobia, biphobia and transphobia, but this isn't enough in itself; we need to be creating inclusive schools that actively celebrate diversity.

My first step into changing the culture at my first school was to get other staff on board. It is not enough to be that one gay teacher. Getting my colleagues on board was important, but it was also important to realise that even LGBT+ allies felt unequipped to deal with the problems ahead.

Standing in front of our staff team on a training day was one thing, but there is nothing more intimidating than your first assembly, let alone one of a 'tough' topic. Hundreds of little faces and eyes glued to your every move and ready for any moment of unease. Assemblies were a great way to spread the message about LGBT+ History Month and, although I didn't know it at the time, they got the ball rolling. Much like others, in the coming weeks, I was greeted on the corridors by a few students I had never spoken to before, occasionally one would come to my door and say, 'I liked your assembly sir'. It was these students who came to our inaugural PRIDE club and helped transform the school.

Having colleagues supporting our endeavours, attend our PRIDE club and speak with our pupils helped show everyone in our school community that at this school, we celebrate diversity. An art teacher ran a project based on LGBT+ activism, we had rainbow cake at a bake sale, school policies were rewritten and staff and students raised money for Stonewall by wearing 'rainbow laces'. All students knew that they had not just one teacher they could speak to but a whole battalion of teachers and support staff who would support them and stamp out discrimination.

Having spoken to other LGBT+ educators, some are concerned about being 'the gay teacher' that is responsible for inclusion. My experience of leading whole school change is reflected in research on the topic by Anna Carlile (2019) who found that before 'inclusion becomes everyone's business' it is often devoted and passionate LGBT+ educators who lead such changes.[2] The long-term impacts of cultural change in schools is something that endures, even if staff move on.

Recently, I had one of those full circle moments when reflecting on my decision to be out in my previous school, when a student in their final year at school responded to a survey. He said:

> Having a role model and someone to speak to made me feel comfortable being out in school; now I get to help other students who have hard time doing the same.

And quite honestly, that makes any challenges I have faced being an 'out' teacher completely worth it and shows that changing the culture of a school truly has a lasting impact.

## Big gay notes from the editor

*Following Allison Zionts' chapter, James Bennett further explores the importance of creating the right culture for LGBT+ staff and young people in schools. The pertinent point to take away from this chapter is 'culture isn't enough to get every child to where they need to go, but if it isn't right, staff and students suffer.' It affects students and staff in terms of achievement, motivation and staff retention and is something that you can feel. We are seeing so many examples across the board of simple and effective ways to create the right culture: Pride clubs, assemblies, open and honest discussion about LGBT+ issues and, of course, visible role models. To change the culture it is necessary to get all of the staff on boar – this isn't just a responsibility that 'the gay teacher' should have to bear alone.*

*Shortly after LGBTed was set up, James was the first trainee teacher I met who had decided to be 'out' from the very beginning of his career. It is great to see that his experiences in two schools have been positive. He argues that children of all backgrounds respect teachers who can teach well, build relationships with them and be open and honest. Being an openly LGBT+ teacher is, therefore, being a good teacher.*

*There are similarities between his school days and my own, showing once again that LGBT+ people have a shared experience of what it feels like to grow up feeling vulnerable and different. We grew with very limited representation of LGBT+ young people in the media – and those we did see were clichéd and negative ones. We had to battle homophobia with very little consequence for the perpetrators.*

*As James identifies, many corporations are significantly ahead of the education sector in enabling LGBT+ people to feel accepted and valued and to perform at their best. We must ask ourselves as teachers and leaders what these major organisations are doing that our schools are not. The students themselves in this chapter are telling us what a difference the small changes can make to their education. As teachers and school leaders, we are too often missing the opportunities that come from our unique position to improve the social mobility of young LGBT+ people.*

## Notes

1. V. Jadva and Stonewall (2017) The Experiences of Lesbian, Gay, Bi and Trans Young People in Britain's Schools in 2017, https://www.stonewall.org.uk/system/files/the_school_report_2017.pdf
2. Anna Carlile (2019) Teacher Experiences of LGBTQ- inclusive Education in Primary Schools Serving Faith Communities in England, UK, Pedagogy. *Culture & Society*, DOI: 10.1080/14681366.2019.1681496

# 10 Bi, Bi, Bi

*Molly Luscombe*

*Molly Luscombe is an English and Media teacher from Wiltshire who describes herself as 'profoundly bisexual'. I think that just about sums it up really.*

### 'When did you come out?'

There is not one answer to this question. There are hundreds: telling my sister, my parents, my friends. Then my uni friends. Then colleagues. Then it's been a decision I've had to make with every new person I've met – figuring out if they'll be cool, or if it'll become a whole 'thing' that I just can't be bothered to deal with for an acquaintance who asks if I have a boyfriend.

When I became a teacher, the question of whether to be 'out' hovered in the back of my mind. What someone does outside of the workplace is their own business, and being bi was unlikely to be relevant in an English lesson, I thought. I wasn't sure about the rules for this, but I thought it could invite problems with colleagues, students or parents. I was new and just wanted to survive.

Many teachers never have to consider this. How many teachers in straight relationships occasionally bring up their spouse or their children casually as part of an anecdote mid-lesson? They are unlikely to be accused of going off track, corrupting young minds or openly discussing their sex lives with children. Nobody is doing that, by the way. That's weird.

Honestly, deep down, I still thought it was inappropriate to discuss queerness with students. Internalised biphobia and the legacy of Section 28 were the cause of this. I know I had queer teachers at school, but it was a secret never to be mentioned. My plan: I wouldn't lie if a student asked me directly, but I would never bring it up. I was comfortably out to colleagues (I taught English and French – insert 'playing for both teams' jokes here), but it remained a secret to students for a while.

On the rare occasion it did come up, the students couldn't have cared less. Usually I'd get an 'Oh. Okay'. Followed by 'Can you help me with this question?' and one slightly misguided 'Don't worry, you don't look gay!' Whatever their reaction, I still felt my heart in my throat as I feared the worst repercussions. I just couldn't stand the idea that someone could accuse me of being unsafe to be around kids. I'd worked so hard to be a teacher and I wasn't secure enough yet to jeopardise it. I didn't just want to be 'that bisexual teacher'. I was determined to establish myself first.

A couple of years after I qualified, a colleague asked if I would mind speaking to one of her sixth formers. I didn't teach this student, so my assumption was that this student was gay and needed someone to talk to. We had a chat over lunch, and I was almost right. I explained to the student that they were safe talking to me about lesbian, gay, bisexual, trans and others (LGBT+) stuff, and that I'm bisexual and that it's nothing to be ashamed of. The student said they definitely liked girls, to which I replied 'Same!' Then the conversation took a slightly unexpected turn.

> The thing is, I've never really felt comfortable as a girl.

My points remained the same: there is nothing wrong with who you are; even if you don't feel ready to come out to everyone just knowing it for yourself is incredible and brave; if you ever need to talk, I'm here. The student cried, I cried afterwards and he has now left school and is living as an openly trans man.

It's still one of the most powerful moments of my career so far.

My head of department, one of the kindest people I know and best leaders I've ever had, stayed in the office adjacent to my classroom for this conversation and spoke to me about it later on. She warned me simply to be careful about telling students too much about myself. 'I mean, I would never tell the kids I'd been on a date!' Well, neither would I. Again, that would be weird. But I couldn't help thinking there must be more students in our school just like this one. Dozens could have been keeping secrets and feeling scared and ashamed about their identity, just like I was at that age – I distinctly remember feeling different to my friends and scared people would think I was strange and I should probably just try to ignore it.

I couldn't bear the idea of any of our kids feeling that way, and I knew I was in a position to do something about it.

Since then, things have escalated quickly, thanks to my incredibly supportive colleagues and the senior leadership team (SLT), and Continuing Professional Development (CPD) from Stonewall and LGBTed. First, I started up SAGA Club (Sexuality and Gender Awareness, so it's not just for LGBT+ students but for allies too). School tightened up policies, I did surveys and delivered training to staff to boost confidence in dealing with homophobia, biphobia and transphobia in school. I've now delivered a handful of assemblies.

In my first assembly, in front of the head, I opened with

> I teach a lot of you. There's loads you probably know about me, and some stuff you might not. I love musicals and reading. I speak French. You're probably all aware that I'm a teacher. Another thing about me is that I happen to be bisexual. None of these things define who I am, but they are all an important part of me.

The head didn't know I was going to say that. I don't think he even knew I was bi, because why would he? He spoke to me about it afterwards to find out what we do in SAGA Club, but he never told me that it was a bad idea to be honest about who I was. And now I know lovely phrases like 'protected characteristic', which mean if anyone tries to tell me to stop I just … won't. And I'll inform my union rep immediately.

Now we have an annual 'Rainbow Day'. Students can wear brightly coloured clothing, face paint, stickers and one has even worn a wig, to show solidarity with their LGBT+ peers.

Even staff get involved. The content of the assemblies ranges from what the different letters in the acronym mean, celebrities/TV characters who identify somewhere in the spectrum of LGBT+, the importance of pronouns, key figures in history who transformed gay and trans rights and the boring stuff about why 'gay' and 'bad' aren't synonyms, to more political ideas with Key Stage 5: how to find out the voting records of Members of Parliaments (MPs), including issues like same-sex marriage and adoption.

We watch videos about LGBT+ children in tutor (I recommend MyGenderation), showing they want the same as everyone else – to be a kid, have fun with their friends, and feel accepted. The students also signed giant rainbow flags, now displayed in reception to show school-wide solidarity. There is some variation in assemblies between year groups, but everyone gets banging tunes.

The overall tone isn't 'if you say this word you will be in *big trouble*'. It's about celebrating all identities. It's about helping students to be as kind to each other as possible. It's about me dancing to Diana Ross while everyone takes a seat.

Some students have rolled their eyes at me in tutor because I'm banging on about gay stuff again. A few still deliberately misgender students because they just don't know how to deal with something they don't understand. Yes, some will still say silly things, but the hard-as-nails Year 11 boys all agreed that if one of their mates came out, they wouldn't have a problem. Nobody has tried to tell me what I'm doing is disgusting or inappropriate, and as far as I know no parents have called the school in a rage. I'm lucky.

Lots of good things *have* happened though:

- Sixth formers have asked if I would go their old schools and do assemblies there, because they'd never seen anything like that before.
- On the last day of school, a girl told me she'd come out to her mum because of my assembly.
- A student made me a mug to say thank you for SAGA Club, and the whole group signed a big rainbow card for me.
- Some of the most vulnerable kids in the school have felt safe and supported by me, by the club and by the ethos of kindness and acceptance in our school.
- A club of kids have sung 'This is Me' from 'The Greatest Showman' in my classroom ….

Would I change the subtler approach of my first couple of years of teaching? Probably not. My students know me as their teacher first and bi second and I'm happy with that. But if I could press a magic button and have the kids think I was straight again, I wouldn't do it. I wish I'd had openly LGBT+ role models at school.

If I've helped just one kid feel a bit better about being themselves, it's worth it.

## Big gay notes from the editor

*'I was new and just wanted to survive'. When Molly became a teacher, she considered the question of whether she wanted to be 'out'. We have all been there. The fact that being 'out' can affect a teacher's credibility, their prospects for promotion and their safety in their role in the 21st century is shameful. And, like Molly, most LGBT+ people have to make the decision whether or not to be 'out' almost every*

*day of our lives, every time we meet a new person or colleague and they happen to ask about relationship status. There is a fundamental difference between bi colleagues and straight ones: the safety of our heterosexual colleagues is not at risk of being fatally undermined if they mention their relationship status.*

*'Don't worry, you don't look gay!' Bi-visibility is about removing the stereotypes and the stigma, and offering reassurance that you will not get into trouble for saying the word. Being 'bi' is particularly challenging and misunderstood, even by many in the LGBT+ community, and bi-erasure is a real problem. By promoting visibility in schools, it shows our young people that 'bi' exists and they do not have to identify as gay or straight. Or anything.*

*The importance of a supportive senior leadership team is once again highlighted in this chapter. When Molly had the affirmation she needed, she was able to make changes across the school for the benefit of LGBT+ young people and have those life-changing conversations with the students who needed it most. As a result of Molly's work, and her visibility as a bisexual person, some of the most vulnerable kids in the school finally felt safe and supported.*

*Reflect on how, as senior leaders, you can support your staff. It is not enough to say you are an 'inclusive school' or a 'diverse school' if your actions do not back it up. If your leadership team is not diverse, then you are not an inclusive school. Having a diverse leadership team is a powerful way to show your staff and students that you value them. If you are not attracting a range of people from different backgrounds, including from across the LGBT+ spectrum, then you are not looking hard enough. I have heard from headteachers who have found that being part of the LGBTed network has attracted candidates to roles that previously would not have come forward. There is a kite mark available from the Centre for LGBTQ+ Inclusion in Education (our partners), which can be awarded to schools that are genuinely inclusive in their work.*

# 11 *That* assembly

*Becca Adson*

*Becca Adson is Head of Year 8 at MEA Central, Manchester, and is a lesbian. In this chapter, she writes about the powerful impact of an assembly she led for International Day Against Homophobia, Biphobia and Transphobia and the other ways in which she has made a difference for lesbian, gay, bisexual, trans and others (LGBT+) students.*

Heart racing, head fuzzy, hands shaking. *You can do this Becca.* I'm in front of 210 Year 7's AND 15 staff. *Just breathe.* What if I mess it up? *You know the lines and you have your cue cards if you forget.* But will I be accepted? ***I think I've got this***.

I take a big deep breath and say "Good morning Year 7".

That assembly was about International Day Against Homophobia, Biphobia and Transphobia (IDAHOBIT), and I was raising awareness of how differently LGBT+ people are treated around the world. I also used it as an opportunity to tell the students that I am a lesbian. When I delivered the line, there was no gasp of surprise or a sea of shocked faces (as I'd feared). At the end of the assembly, my headteacher simply walked down the theatre steps and gave me a huge hug in front of all the students. Such a small gesture had such a huge impact and many other teachers offered similar support. As I stood on the door, wishing students a great day as they left, many of them smiled but then something quite special happened. Two students told me they needed to speak with me quite urgently. They were the first two students who told me they were LGBT+ and, in the 18 months since, more have done the same.

In the five short years since my teacher training, a lot has changed. Or, perhaps, I have changed. On my first placement, I was so scared to admit I had a girlfriend that I lied and told my mentor I was single (I'll never forget when she tried to set me up with her son!). In my first teaching school, I talked about my "partner", always saying "they" when referring to my now wife. When we were out in town, I'd always look around in case anyone saw us, terrified the school rumour mill would start. It was when I moved to my second school after three years, that my mind started to shift. I decided then that I didn't want to hide who I was, but I had no idea how to go about being my true, authentic self as a teacher. Other (straight) teachers made it look so easy, referring to their husband or wife during lessons, or in conversations with children – would I ever get to that point?

I started small, I came out to staff slowly, they seemed supportive and so I plucked up the courage to tell my best class. Again, they were fine, probably a little stunned to silence or maybe they just didn't really care! Then I started to get student visitors at my door each day;

news travels fast in Manchester secondary schools! Some were clarifying the rumour that they had heard: "Miss are you really a lesbian?! But you don't look like a lesbian!" Others just wanted to know how my day was, or what I had been up to at the weekend. These students later came out as LGBT+, and as they became more confident, I became their number one source of advice on all things LGBT+.

Another big turning point came when the school's Personal, Social and Health Education (PSHE) leader asked me to support her with a government-funded, LGBT inclusion award called the Rainbow Flag Award (RFA), run by the Proud Trust (a Manchester-based LGBT+ charity). Finally, it felt as though I could use the (hideous) experience when I was a student in school to make my little part of the world more inclusive to students like me.

At a time that I was working on my own confidence as a lesbian teacher, I was also trying to understand the struggles of LGBT+ students who have very different experiences from my own. I was lucky that my parents were so supportive and the LGBT+ community has been very welcoming, but I quickly found this wasn't the case for everyone, particularly for many of the black and minority ethnic (BAME) pupils at the school. I was desperate to give these students a role model that they could truly relate to and so trawled the internet for inspiration and contacted the ever-supportive Proud Trust and Chloe Cousins (the BAME lead) who gave me a wealth of information that I could use.

The RFA was a lot of work. School red tape meant progress was sometimes slow and I didn't always have ownership of the work I wanted to do, but I was able to deliver training to staff, host a small, whole school Pride event and make meaningful change to whole school policy. Staff began asking me for support with LGBT+ students and other LGBT+ staff started to feel comfortable in coming out; the change in culture was staggering in such a short space of time. I also set up an LGBT+ and allies staff network, we met every half term and discussed ideas or initiatives and we acted as a support network for when times were tough.

I realised that I was good at helping others who felt they didn't fit in, and my passion was in the "fluffy" stuff that didn't directly boost our position in the national league tables. My passion was the students, not necessarily the grades they achieved. So, after a year at the school, I had a massive career change. I went from a classroom teacher to a Head of Year at a brand-new school called MEA Central.

I started after the Easter holidays and at the time, they only had 210 Year seven pupils. I'd sat in my interview for the role wondering where my new confidence had come from. I told my prospective employers that I was a lesbian and I wanted to use my experiences to support students. I also told them that I would like to lead on the RFA to create a truly inclusive environment in their growing school.

To my delight, they offered me the position and I grabbed it with both hands. It was a big change, and the school's core vision is "A fantastic future for all" with a huge focus on accelerated progress and above expected GCSE grades; my role would be to remove barriers that stop children accessing lessons.

At Central, I wanted my coming out experience to be different. I didn't want my sexuality to be gossip, like at my previous school, but to be normalised from day one. I knew IDAHO-BIT was coming up, and when I floated the idea of a coming out assembly, my line manager was extremely supportive. I spent hours making my PowerPoint and rehearsed it so many times at home; my wife knew almost every word! I'd included in my assembly examples of faraway countries where being LGBT+ is punishable by law but introduced them by saying "if my wife and I lived here, this is what would happen to us".

I later went on to submit this assembly as evidence for the RFA and the feedback from Rachel Williams (the RFA lead at the Proud Trust) was wonderful: "So many schools make this a distant thing – it happens to other people. Using yourself here in such a positive way says so clearly to students – this is here, this is us".

We have since passed all sections of the RFA (one of only three secondary schools to do so in the first try in Manchester), and LGBT+ inclusion is woven into the fabric of our school as it grows. One of our school values is Citizenship which we simply call "be kind" and our students absolutely embody this. I receive pictures drawn by students almost weekly, all featuring rainbows or having LGBT written on them. I have received presents from students for being "my true self" and supportive emails from parents. I cried with joy when we celebrated LGBT+ History Month by taking a day off timetable to hold a Central Pride – seeing the students learn about Marsha P Johnson and write letters to Alan Turing was just overwhelming. The feeling that I did this, fully supported by my amazing team of teachers, leaders, parents and students, cannot be compared.

I never thought I would work in place, where I could just be my authentic, true self without fear of prejudice or hate. The support I have received has been truly fantastic, but the real joy comes from seeing trans students able to be themselves and access lessons without fear; bisexual students coming out to their friends and family or seeing young allies emerge in front of my eyes.

When I reflect on how far I have come on this journey, I wish I could go back to my PGCE self and tell her what was to come; you can do this, and it will all be worth it. Or go back to before *that* assembly and assure myself that not only have I got this, not only will I be accepted, but I will also get to see so many staff and students benefit from my visibility. They would inspire me enough to do it all over again.

I would have said, be confident, find your support network in school and use them. Speak to your senior leadership team (SLT), if they don't have your back – find a school that does. An educator is in the unique position where their actions can and do have a direct influence on young people. Your actions will make or break a students' experience of school, so be brave and be you.

Twitter: @MrsAdsonMEAC

## Big gay notes from the editor

*There is no one "correct" way to be an "out" teacher, but this chapter offers another example of why assemblies can be effective. They offer a clear, consistent message to all students at once that all students are valued. Becca's advice is to be confident, find your support network in your school and use them.*

*She states that supporting LGBT+ inclusion in schools is often considered to be the "fluffy stuff" that does not necessarily contribute to league tables. However, at the 2019 Stonewall Conference, Ofsted Chief Inspector Amanda Spielman said,*

*it's vital all children are taught about the wonderful diversity of humanity in modern Britain: a diversity of race, gender, faith and love... teachers, schools and young people's services should create inclusive environments where all young people are to reach their full potential.*[1]

*Therefore, there is a requirement to support our LGBT+ students in this way. As I said in Chapter 1, how can students be expected to access a currirulum if they don't feel safe in school? Becca has found ways in her role to remove barriers that children have when accessing lessons.*

*Of course, there are many other ways to 'usualise' LGBT+ visibility in schools. In Chapter 12, Callum Richardson channels Gandalf to show how it is the little acts of kindness and love that can benefit our LGBT+ students most.*

## Note

1 https://www.stonewall.org.uk/about-us/news/ofsted-chief-says-schools-should-celebrate-diversity-stonewall-conference

# 12 Simple acts of kindness and love

*Callum Richardson*

*Callum Richardson is a history teacher, who began his Newly Qualified Teacher year at a school in London in September 2020. Before this he worked as a learning support mentor in the north east, subsequently completing his training there also. In this chapter, Callum shares a series of small exchanges he has had with students about his sexuality, exploring the fear that LGBT+ teachers feel about losing the positive relationships they have with students as a result of coming out.*

Last year I worked as a Learning Support Mentor in a mainstream school Special Educational Needs (SEN) department. Aside from SEN, our department also helped children with English as an Additional Language access the curriculum. Despite being young, it being my first role within a classroom and with me being in a school with a high proportion of faith students, it was important for me to be honest about my sexuality.

I was a late Section 28 child, and although it was repealed in my last few years of primary school, I still grew up in an environment where being "gay" still just wasn't addressed – sadly, neither was the bullying. LGBT+ relationships simply weren't on the curriculum. Even if they were, I doubt many teachers would have felt comfortable delivering it; the residual effect of that cruel act still is firm in their heads. Being a working class boy, growing up in an economically disadvantaged part of the North East, it was unsurprising that I had few role models in which to look up to. LGBT+ people weren't as visible in the early 2000s, unsurprisingly considering the internet was in its infancy; with no Facebook, Twitter, Instagram or YouTube to connect or share stories – a fact many people overlook these days.

Throughout my time in education, from primary school right up until university, I was not taught by a single openly LGBT+ member of staff. Were there rumours? Yes. Have I since found out that I was indeed taught by LGBT+ teachers? Yes. Do I feel bitter that my time in education could have been made better by a teacher being "out"? Only slightly. Instead my overwhelming emotion towards these teachers, to whom still continued to inspire me and deliver a first-class education, is pity. Pity that they felt as though they had to hide something so crucial about themselves. As cis heterosexual members of staff would gladly share small parts of their life, such as a wedding or an upcoming pregnancy, their desk is neatly adorned with the pictures of their loved ones. I can't imagine the tension LGBT+ teachers must have felt, probably very similar to my own at the time, of being officially "outed" to the student population. I also wonder whether the support would have even been there for staff, should they have made the leap. Given homophobic bullying was rife throughout the student part of the community, I'm inclined to believe not.

So given my own experience, the idea of me being an out teacher, when the time came to have a class of my own, was always my intention. "Be who you needed when you were at school". This phrase is used a lot, but I definitely feel as though there is truth in what it seeks to inspire. The idea that a deeply closeted child has the opportunity to see, in "the real world", a successful and positive role model always filled me with optimism. Likewise the opportunity to normalise the community for heterosexual students, who may one day begin to question their own identity or, more likely, have LGBT+ children of their own, was equally as important – as a community, we've gone beyond just preaching to the choir.

It took a while for the topic to come up with a student. However, it was inevitable given the fact that another female teacher, who was married, shared my second name. I never raised the issue directly myself, and I always allowed the students and staff to ask in their own time. That part was important to me, as I feel it's important to normalise LGBT+ people in society – labels are for the comfort of other people. I just continued on with my life as I would, inside or outside the classroom.

The first time I come out to a class was just before Christmas, a couple of months into my role. The topic had not yet even come up with my colleagues, though I suspect they already knew and were not too sure how to approach the topic. The class was just beginning and they were curious, being inquisitive year nines, as to whether myself and a female colleague of mine were in a relationship. The truth was that we were close friends, having started mere weeks apart and being the same age. Having a long-term partner herself, she politely said no. To which one of the girls asked me, "Are you in a relationship Sir?" I answered yes. "Is it your wife?" I answered no. "Your girlfriend then?" Again, I answered no, to which the girl appeared completely confused. "How can you be in a relationship but not have a wife or girlfriend?" My colleagues smiling, having the truth confirmed for them, looked at me and then the student. "Sir doesn't have a wife, he doesn't have a girlfriend but is in a relationship. Think about it." It was then that the penny eventually dropped and, for just a moment, I returned to the same feeling I had when I came out for the first time. The idea that a secret, one I've maintained for so long, is finally out in the open. It's an odd kind of loss. It took a few moments to remind myself that this was ok, I was in a safe space and I had indeed done this before.

Naturally, the class was inquisitive. However, the best part for me was the way in which they reacted. It wasn't disgust, and none of them made a big scene, instead their most vocal reaction was a short "Oh". That in itself meant the world to me. That small reaction was anything anyone could want when coming out. Not to be treated, nor viewed, any differently than several seconds previous. It also reminded me just how far society had come since my time at school, as I know for a fact that if one of my LGBT+ teachers came out, the reactions of my fellow pupils would not have been so subdued.

However, the time I feel I did the most good, as an LGBT+ figure, was during a mixed ability year eight English intervention. The session was drawing to a close, as was the end of the day, so the students were slowly packing up, ready to go home. It was at that point when a conversation, between two of the girls in the class, was overheard. She was talking about being bisexual, so naturally the response of the boy who overheard was to make a big scene questioning this. There was no malice I must add; he was simply curious. A little back and forth was had, as she talked a little about it, at which point one of the girls said "Well, Sir's gay". She has obviously heard about me from another student in my year nine class.

Everyone in the room appeared to take this well, merely shrugging it off and returning to packing up. Despite this, one boy's eyes quickly darted to me in confusion. He was an EAL student, who was very open about his faith. He had previously described me as his "favourite teacher", so I'd be lying if I didn't say I was concerned at the prospect of that changing. He approached my desk tentatively and asked, "Sir. So my mum and dad, a man and a woman, love each other. For you, it is a man and a man?" I remember this conversation clear as day, as he was using his fingers to explain – his index fingers each representing the individual parties invoked. I simply replied yes – that is the case.

Although being an educator and not one to miss an opportunity, I reminded the class that everyone should feel safe at school. Being horrible to someone about their religion was just as bad as being horrible about sexuality – it was in fact a crime. All of the students took this on board, with the girls in question thanking me. Thankfully the EAL student didn't appear fazed by my sexuality, and he even continued to refer to me as his favourite teacher.

During my remaining time at the school, I had a few more encounters being "outed" as a teacher. Students would approach me, nervously in a lesson, saying they had heard another student mention that I'm gay. I would always reply the same way, saying that was indeed the case. The best reaction I overheard from this was when one student returned to his table. He was quick to tell the boy who sat next to him, whose response to this was "So what? It doesn't make a difference".

Though it may not be as fast as we would like, it appears society is starting to change. Students and staff are finally beginning to feel comfortable being their true self – something a million miles away from anything this closeted, quiet boy could have imagined back in the early 2000s. As LGBT+ educators, we have a responsibility to stand on the shoulders of our forebears. To be out, it is not just for the students and staff of today but for those who have long since left education.

As Gandolf describes in *The Hobbit*, it is the small everyday things such as simple acts of kindness that keep the darkness away.

## Big gay notes from the editor

*We are seeing time and time again the spectre of Section 28 rearing its ugly head. Numerous teachers have been impacted profoundly by it, either as an LGBT+ child in school or as a teacher. The idea that we can gradually overcome this with simple acts of kindness and love is a beautiful one: those small exchanges in the classroom which "usualise" LGBT+ people will have the biggest impact. However, many LGBT+ teachers fear that these exchanges in which they are "outed" will result in a loss of respect from pupils and colleagues.*

*Bravely "out" from the beginning of his career, Callum's experience was a positive one like so many others in this collection. We all share with him the sense of relief when we are finally "out", when the reaction, where it even exists, is good. We also share the fear of it all going horribly wrong.*

*Callum writes about his naturally inquisitive students, "the class was just beginning and they were curious, being inquisitive year nines, as to whether myself and a female colleague of mine were in a relationship". Be honest, how many LGBT+ colleagues have "played along" when assumptions have been made about their heterosexuality in order to feel safer, particularly in the early part of their career? In my Newly Qualified Teacher year, I was in a very close friendship with a female colleague. Gossip was rife amongst students about us being in a relationship. We danced together at prom and let them think what they wanted …*

Callum writes, "the idea that a deeply closeted child has the opportunity to see, in 'the real world', a successful and positive role model always filled me with optimism". Young people have a love of learning and will often ask questions. As a visible LGBT+ role model, it is so important not to miss opportunities to answer these questions. Students should not fear asking them and teachers should not fear answering them. With each honest answer, each small act of kindness, we move closer to being our authentic selves and making our schools genuinely great places for our LGBT+ young people.

Once again, the students in this chapter show themselves to be open-minded, non-judgemental and kind. We as adults can learn a lot from them.

# 13 Add a little bit of glitter
*Faye Cutting*

*Secondary Modern Foreign Languages teacher Faye Cutting, with 22 years' experience, is a visionary Personal Social and Health Education lead. She has a passion for acceptance and diversity, chocolate and cheesecake, rainbows and glitter, her wife and their daughter.*

As yet another teacher who has been through education under the shadow of Section 28, I hadn't realised that the female PE teacher I 'idolised', I was actually probably attracted to! And once I'd started teaching I found it hard to let my 'true self' show ... to begin with. I had a Year 12 boy in my form who was clearly gay, the day he came in wearing a straw boater, à la traditional ice cream seller, his sexuality was clear to me – and my gaydar – long before he came to have a chat with me. I guess he'd 'known' about me and felt safe to share his story with me.

From then on, I made a pact with myself: not necessarily to be 'out and proud', as this is not my style, but just honest with my students. If they asked me if my husband liked football, "no but my wife does" would be my reply. The first time I said it, my heart was beating out of my chest, cartoon style, but nothing changed. I realised it didn't change anything negatively for me and started some excellent conversations, especially when I entered a civil partnership with my wife. Talking about the wedding, one of my forms wanted to know 'how it worked', and I thought he meant how *it* worked (shudder) but he just wanted to know who walked who down the aisle ...

I started doing some lesbian, gay, bisexual, trans and others (LGBT+) diversity work at my school, and I came across a blog from a former student who had struggled with her sexuality as a student 'as there were no LGBT+ role models in my life', she wrote, 'there were no LGBT+ teachers that I knew of, though I knew they must have been there'. Yes, yes, *yes* I was, I had been there! This student suffered from anorexia as it was the only part of her life she could control as she was in such turmoil about her sexuality. I wish I had known, perhaps sharing my story and being the role model she never had, that I had never had, may have helped.

A new form came along, and so therefore did the need to 'out' myself once more – I can't stand that phrase – where have I been in? I've not been hiding, just as a teacher I felt torn between keeping my private life 'private' and being authentic. Quite early on, I told them about my wife and expected there to be massive ripples and a spreading of this news. Once again, as I told the first few students in front of me, I expected a clap of thunder, an earthquake, to be struck by lightening, but no nothing at all. It was so 'ordinary' to them. But then, a totally heart-warming, reaffirming moment occurred, two girls asked to talk to me at break time, the way they do when there's an issue with another teacher, or they've started their periods, and all they wanted to say was 'We wanted to say we thought you were brave telling us and it makes no difference to us, we still love you!' We still love you?!?! Wholly mackerel, this was just one of the best things a student has said to me in 20 years of teaching. And it made me reflect on my not so positive experience, when I had first started teaching.

Now, remember, that times have changed considerably and now it would be highly unlikely for kids to yell 'Lezzie' during a lesson every time your back is turned, or to have the indecency to tippex, yes tippex, lesbian on your classroom wall or to yell at you in the street. But those words, 'we still love you', became my overriding memory of being 'out' to the students.

It was then I knew I needed to do more. An MFL teacher by trade, I started using more examples of same-sex parents in my examples – Christophe a deux mères, ses parents, elles travaillent . . . and having those conversations that some people DO have two mums or two dads, in the same way that someone may live with a carer or grandparent; to 'normalise' the situation – God I hate that – *normal*, what *is* normal? We are *all* unique! I ordered some posters, from an LGBT+ charity, telling people to get over the fact that some people are gay, bisexual, transgender, etc. I expected the posters to get pulled down or defaced in some way, but nope! Not a negative reaction to be seen or heard!

My 'we still love you' form were now heading towards the end of year 8, and a lad in my form came to tell me he thought he was gay. So, we had a 'school mum, school son' chat about his feelings and whether or not his family knew. He said he'd told them, but they'd asked him not to tell his grandparents. I reassured him that this was not because they were ashamed of him, just that grandparents were from another era and may not understand so easily. We spoke of how he could tell his friends and if he wanted to speak to the Head of Year in terms of getting him emotional support. He asked me to. *Huge!* This was me, this was my impact . . . a student came to me, yes *me*, but why me?? In a subsequent meeting with the parents of said student, the parents thanked me. What for? Being a dedicated form tutor, for my hard work, for encouraging him to take part in Sports day and house events? No, for being me. For talking about my life with my wife, and daughter, by this point. His mum said how he would come home and talk about me over dinner. A slightly uncomfortable thought, though she went on to say that without me sharing my experiences and talking about my family that she didn't feel he would have been able to talk to her and her husband about the way he was feeling. She said she would be ever grateful for that. Now, I wasn't at that meeting, but the Head of Year came to find me straight away to tell me. God, financially, if I had been able I would have resigned there and then, job done!!

Spurred on once more by this, and with a responsibility role change into PSHEE lead of our large, secondary school, I felt empowered to make more of a difference. I began working on raising understanding and acceptance of LGBT+ staff and students in our school, by adding further LGBT+ examples into the PSHEE sessions which I planned and by adjusting the wording in our RSE (Relationships and Sex Education) policy and sessions, because otherwise there was a whole section of our school population who we were failing. Yes, failing! Sex is not only heterosexual sex and nor are our students. Remember, we are not teaching how to be gay, but how to be safe – because 'gayness' cannot be taught. We teach about Romans in school but no one becomes roman and starts feeding their enemies to the lions. We are simply creating an inclusive, safe place for all of our students. And *that* is what matters!

By being more 'visible' I had a student teacher, in some observations in our department, ask to speak with me. He was worried about going to his first job, at a neighbouring Catholic school, and he didn't know whether or not to hide who he was. 'Hell no!' came my reply; we need to be there for the students, who like us when we were at school, were trying to work out why we were different or why we idolised our PE teachers, we need to be those examples of how being LGBT+ doesn't harm your life or your career. It brings its challenges, but surely challenges are what life is about and all our differences are what makes us the same, aren't they?

I have worked to obtain a recognised accreditation for our work as a school for being a safe, inclusive place for students and staff alike, and I give training on tackling HBT (homophobic, biphobic, transphobic) bullying, empowering our staff to tackle those oh so damaging little comments, such as 'that's so gay' and 'err lezzer'. I recently dealt with a couple of Year 7 students who felt it was ok to insult each other by saying they had 'gay' haircuts! I spoke to them out of the room and asked them to tell me what a gay haircut looked like as I *really* needed to know?!? I made my point about other people's feelings and how damaging such 'insults' could be.

Staff now come to me for advice on LGBT+ issues, and we have a school environment where two year 10 girls feel safe to walk around holding hands. I am on the Transgender Working Party, and I am now revamping our RSE policy, framework and sessions to ensure that they meet the new statutory requirements. We hold a diversity week each year, we have a range of LGBT+ books in the library (with which we were unable to make a display this year, as they were all booked out!) and we fly the Pride flags with glee. I even put on a screening of 'Love Simon', the coming of age/coming out movie. I expected maybe 20 students to show up and was overwhelmed when over 200 came, and I had to call for extra help supervising them all!

Now I cannot claim responsibility for the overwhelming positive attitude in my school, but I do know that being who I am is helping. There are those that I know I have helped and hopefully many more. We are starting an LGBT+ support group soon to give the pupils more of a voice. I'm nothing special, just a 40 something, teacher, married with a four-year-old daughter whom we idolise, living my life, being the best role model I can be, making a difference with a little bit of rainbow glitter!

## Big gay notes from the editor

*Being a visible LGBT+ teacher has a fantastic ripple effect. You become the teacher that your colleagues and students go to for advice about LGBT+ issues. This is all very rewarding but is also quite exhausting. It is not only the responsibility of 'the gay teacher' to support LGBT+ inclusion in the school. We all need allies amongst the staff body – especially on the leadership team.*

*In this chapter, Faye writes about finding a balance between keeping your private life private and being a visible and authentic role model. This has come up from so many teachers I have met: they have been told that they should not share any aspect of their private lives with the students (but it is usually only the LGBT+ teachers that are told this). One such exchange was 'well, if you wouldn't tell them you are hungover, why would you tell them you are married to someone of the same sex?' This is an utterly ridiculous false equivalence similar to what comes up time and time again, usually from right-wing mouthpieces on radio stations. It is never professional or appropriate to talk to students about your drunken antics at the weekend, nor your sex life, but why would it not be acceptable to show young people that LGBT+ people can be happily married?*

*Faye also tells us of a time when she missed an opportunity to help a student who had been anorexic as a result of her battle with her sexuality. In the opening chapter, I asked you to consider when you may have missed an opportunity and what you would have done differently. It's very clear that in this situation that even a conversation with a teacher would have helped. By being visible and authentic, we show our students that it is possible to be 'different' and be successful at the same time. With a little bit of glitter, we can show LGBT+ students it gets better. They need to know this. I know I did.*

# 14 'Miss, I'm part of LGBT too'
*Amy Ridler*

*Amy Ridler is a writer and trainee English teacher in London. She is also a tattooed feminist theatre collaborator and queer literature enthusiast.*

When I was at school, I was unsure of my sexuality. I knew there had been women I had really *really* liked: a few teachers, my next door neighbour's decorator (that I had felt drawn to when she would stand on our communal balcony to smoke) and … Celine Dion. But I had no idea why. I'd talk about boys with my friends and even had boyfriends, but I never got the 'hype' around them. It was just something you did, just like everyone else.

I was lucky enough to have been taught by many brilliant and inspiring women at secondary school, but one really stood out to me from the first day. Our music teacher. She was instantly one of my favourite teachers, and I joined the school choir even though I was awkward and used to stand at the back and mime. I think she knew but took pity on me. I didn't have a crush on her, but there was something that made me want to be around her as much as possible in school. As the term went on, I learnt that she was a fellow pupil's *other* mum. She was married to the pupil's biological mum. I found this fascinating and took every opportunity to attend the parties of this pupil in order to catch glimpses of their household. This woman's identity was so authentic that it was never discussed or questioned, it just was. Years after I left school, I came out. When I decided I wanted to teach, I planned to make sure I was visible and unapologetic about my identity. She was unaware at the time, but just by being herself and present in my education, that teacher shaped part of my story when I think back to how I processed my sexuality.

At the first school I worked at, the proportion of lesbian, gay, bisexual, trans and others (LGBT+) staff members was much higher than any other I have been at to date. This made being out at work very natural and easy. From teaching assistants, right through to heads of department and members of SLT, there was LGBT+ representation and visibility.

After I left the school to move from special education to Secondary English, I started working at an alternative provision in a different borough. This school was completely different from my previous school. The team members were so welcoming and friendly – there was no hostility, but I had gone from working in an extremely diverse and large school with over a hundred members of staff, to a very small and close knit team of 20. As I got to know the staff, it became apparent that I was the only person who identified as LGBT+ and I had not spoken about my private life so was, thus far, invisible.

At lunch times, the staff and pupils would eat together and I remember one lunch time: I was sat with a group of particularly loud students and a history teacher. She was telling me all about her wedding plans and I thought to myself, 'right-now is the time to drop it into conversation.' (It seems ridiculous now that I would feel the need to *drop it* into conversation, but this was my thought process at the time!) I mentioned my partner and continued on with whatever anecdote I was telling, assuming that the choice of the word partner rather than boyfriend would have been enough. I was wrong of course, and the first question she asked was where *he* lived. At that point I could have corrected her, but for some reason, I just answered the question, finished my lunch and the conversation and left the table.

When I got home that night, I was really annoyed at myself. Why was I acting ashamed of who I was? Since I had come out, I had been unapologetically proud and now for some reason, in this new setting, I was hiding.

There was no opportunity to speak about my private life to staff members for a while after that as the job was quite demanding and hands-on. I had been given a number of students to work 1:1 with on their reading. I was quite apprehensive about one of the girls I had been assigned as she displayed a lot of very challenging behaviour throughout the school day. In the first few sessions we had in the library, I just about got her to sit down and listen to me read a paragraph or two before her attention would be drawn to whatever was happening in the hall, or with another student in a different classroom. I persevered and asked her to write down three things she liked – I had decided to first get her interested in the reading by finding articles or poems about things she liked, before we stood a chance at finishing 'Holes'! She handed it back to me in silence – she wasn't a big talker – at the end of the day. On her list she had written, 1. Pink 2. Pink 3. Pink.

At first glance I thought, 'OK well she hasn't given it much thought but her favourite colour is pink, so that's a start.' The next day I had printed an article about a woman who only ever wears pink, ready for our next session. As we finished reading the article, one line each, she turned to me and said, 'Miss, thanks for finding that for me but I meant Pink the singer. I love her.' We laughed about it and I said I would come much better prepared for our next meeting.

One afternoon, we were sitting in the library. I was just congratulating her on the work she had produced when she pointed to the sorry looking LGBT+ display board and said to me, 'Miss, are you part of LGBT?' It really took me by surprise and I thought it was so sweet the way she had said 'part of' like it was a special club. My first thought was 'Am I allowed to discuss my sexuality with the pupils?' Then I thought about how many times a day I had heard other staff members referring to their wives or husbands and thought – Now *is* the time. I said yes and a look of relief came over her face, and probably over mine too. The lunch bell rang, and she got up and left. That was it. I sat there looking at tatty cut-outs of a very young Ellen DeGeneres and Elton John smiling down from the display board.

For the next week or so, she became more focused in our sessions. We had gone from me pleading with her to even sit down with her coat off, to her reading aloud to me from various articles I could find about Pink and then onto reading the text she was meant to be, along with her classmates. I knew that telling her that I was a lesbian had had an effect on her, but I didn't want to ask her anything that may influence her or rock the boat. I was just happy with the progress she had made. About a week after she had asked me that question, she was walking out of our session, and as she got to the door, she turned and said, 'Miss, I'm part of LGBT too' and then walked out. I still think about that day and how hard it would be for a 14-year-old girl in the environment she was in, both at school and at home, to have had the strength to say that to a teacher.

The LGBT+ display board had been irking me since I had started at the school. By no means am I denying that both Ellen and Elton are key figures, but they are in no way representative of the demographic of the pupils in the school; I wasn't sure that 90% of the students could even name them. The board was quite bare and the rest was taken up with helplines – again, important but slightly depressing. There was no celebratory element. I decided I would re-do the display board to bring it back to life and was given the go ahead by the headteacher. I asked the student if she would like to help me and let her know that she was in no way obliged as this would be in her free time. She was in. She even went as far as to take paper and borrow school paints to make a rainbow banner for the top of the board over the weekend. We assembled the board over lunchtimes – she sat ferociously cutting out pictures of Samira Wiley, Frank Ocean, Olly Alexander and Laverne Cox – we kept Ellen and Elton, of course, but updated their photos. We did a section about Pride marches across the world and kept the helpline information, but made the theme a celebration of LGBT+ identity. One afternoon I heard a group of pupils say to her, 'If you're making that board with Miss, does that mean you're gay?' I had worried that negativity from her peers may have ruined all positivity she had been displaying, but she said to them, 'Yes. I think so. I am right now anyway.' I think the honest and unapologetic way that she answered them made it harder for them to tease her, which was my fear, so they just accepted it. She became more and more chatty and the very quiet girl who was known for walking out of class at the drop of a hat with no explanation and was suddenly not only completing her work but also taking pride in it. The positive impact that my visibility had on that pupil reminded me how important it is to be authentic and to make sure that you are visible and proud of your identity, especially when around pupils who look up to you.

I now work at a different school, and I am 'out.' I wear a small rainbow pin on my lanyard at all times so as to stay visible to all pupils. Not only is this a way of volunteering myself as someone to approach if a pupil wants to speak to an LGBT+ member of staff, but the prospect of having to ask is too daunting, but also as a constant reminder to myself that I am proud of who I am. I am proud to be in a career in which I can support LGBT+ young people. For some of them, I will be the first person that they choose to speak to about their sexuality.

## Big gay notes from the editor

*The simple message of this chapter is this: by being visible, young people can identify with you. Amy looked up to one of her teachers and this inspired her many years later to be an 'out' teacher. In the same way, young people may look for somebody with the same ethnicity as them or look up to their favourite musician or music teacher. You can't be what you can't see. The photographs on display boards of Elton John and Ellen DeGeneres are all well and good – and certainly a step in the right direction – but these celebrities do not reflect the school community. Schools must seek to reflect their community in the staff body and the leadership team.*

*The idea of having an identity so authentic that it isn't even discussed is a compelling one. As teachers, how often have we admired that colleague's instinctive grasp of behaviour management or command of a room and wondered how they do it? For LGBT+ students, we can be that teacher by being visible and unapologetic about our identity. LGBT+ teachers can help shape students' identities – whether it be a love of sport, a talent for music or finding your place in the world as an LGBT+ person.*

*'Volunteering ourselves' as that person students can turn to can be life-changing, and in the next chapter, Hadley Stewart writes about what it is like being taught by 'that' teacher.*

# 15 The cupboard without a rainbow flag

*Hadley Stewart*

*Hadley Stewart has written for Attitude, BuzzFeed, Euronews, FS, Gay Star News, NBC News, PinkNews, The Queerness, Reuters, and several other publications. His essay exploring his experiences of being gay in an all-boys' school, 'Masculinity and Homosexuality in School', is published in the Amazon best-selling book,* Boys Don't Try? Rethinking Masculinity in Schools.

There was no rainbow flag across the door of B39, the classroom that most of our A-level English classes took place. But I knew I was accepted there. I call it a classroom, but it was almost too small to fit the ten students of our class. The windows didn't open properly, which in a school full of sweaty teenage boys was particularly problematic. During winter it was too cold, and during summer too hot. A table ran across the middle of the room, with five students on each side, at the head of the table, was our English teacher, a true ally of the lesbian, gay, bisexual, trans and others (LGBT+) community. B39 is no longer there; not the B39 we knew. It is now a cupboard. Nevertheless, it was our cupboard. And whilst the table might have been removed and the walls painted another colour, the legacy of B39 lives on today.

I left school five years ago. It was there where I came out as gay to my friends and cried in the toilets when people would call me names for it. The first few years were tough. Everybody 'knew' I was gay before I did, and they wouldn't make any secret of it. I wasn't the stereotypical school boy to say the least. I was camp, hated sport, liked writing. And fancied boys. It didn't bother me too much, being different. I mean, my name is Hadley, and I've always felt a bit different from the rest of the crowd. But going from a mixed primary school to an all-boys' school, I soon realised that I didn't entirely fit in.

I would hear the word 'gay' being used on a daily basis. It would often be used to mean that something was broken, wrong or disgusting. Not exactly what I wanted to hear as I was figuring out who I was. The word was dripping with shame and embarassment. When I'd finally figured out that I was gay, it would take me years to feel comfortable to use the word 'gay' to describe my own sexuality. Decades before I was born, another gay alumnus was working out who he was at a time when it was illegal to be gay. Sir Ian McKellen, arguably the most famous and influential gay man on the planet, walked the same halls as I did on his first day at school. He is a talented actor and fearless LGBT+ rights activist, yet the latter was seldom mentioned whenever teachers would talk about him. It was made clear to me that the school wasn't comfortable talking about gay people.

A turning point in my school life would come in Year 12 as I entered B39. Our teacher was a Madonna fan; Madge's music would sometimes provide a musical accompaniment, as we discussed how gender is a social construct or analysed the lyrics of 'Like a Prayer' for innuendo. At an all-boys' school, this seemed somewhat ground-breaking. Madonna rebelled against the status quo and so did our English teacher. As an ally of the LGBT+ community when very few in the public eye were, Madonna set the tone of what the rest of society should be doing when it came to fighting for our community's civil rights. I view my English teacher in this way too. During my time at school, not many teachers would jump to the defence of their queer students, whereas she wouldn't hesitate. She was a bit of a trailblazer in that sense. Things are fortunately changing at my former school, but I can't help but wonder if things would have been better for myself and other LGBT+ students had we had more visible allies.

I feel extremely fortunate to have come across a teacher like her, because I know that not every LGBT+ young person benefits from such a role model. When I was struggling with my own sexuality, a few years before attending my first English A-level class, I came across a YouTube project that showed me I wasn't alone in this struggle. The It Gets Better Project allowed LGBT+ people from across the world to post their messages of inspiration, heartbreak and self-discovery with a global audience, many of whom were young queer people feeling isolated. The rates of poor mental health amongst LGBT+ young people remain disproportionately high, with risk factors influencing these trends including social isolation, feeling different and discrimination. This is just another example of why challenging discriminatory behaviour towards LGBT+ students is so important.

My deputy headteacher led an assembly about the impact that bullying can have on those who experience it. He spoke about Tyler Clementi, a young gay man living in New York City. Tyler died by suicide after facing a torrent of homophobic abuse from his university roommate. He was just 18. I remember sitting in the assembly, my cheeks felt like they were on fire, as I fought hard to stop tears from rolling down them. That evening, I went home and cried. I knew that I too had felt like there was nobody I could talk to about being gay. I felt grief at the loss of so many young LGBT+ lives. I felt anger at the people who had passively stood by, unchallenging the torment that many of these young people had gone through. The need to have positive LGBT+ role models and visible allies for young people can have a life-saving impact. The narrative of 'sticks and stones' needs to end. LGBT+ young people deserve better from our education system.

This generation of young people are arguably the most socially conscious and politically aware teenagers since the 1960s. It would be a disservice to them that LGBT+ topics are not discussed within their classroom. After all, they will all know, or know of, an LGBT+ person. I remain baffled every time I hear adults talking about what children should and shouldn't know about the world they're growing up in, completely oblivious of the fact that these young people know and understand a lot more than what we're giving them credit for. I suspect most young people know that LGBT+ people exist, but it's how they are viewed in their home environment and local community that will influence the narrative around our community in wider society.

But I can see why LGBT+ teachers and those who consider themselves as allies of our community would feel nervous at the thought of 'coming out' in their school. We only have to look at the recent protests outside primary schools in Birmingham to feel the lack of support for LGBT+ people from those at the Department of Education and further afield. I don't blame any LGBT+ teacher for not feeling able to be themselves in the classroom, because like any other LGBT+ person, I too have shied away from questions about my sexuality in situations where I've felt threatened. Yet sometimes we have to step up and ask ourselves, if we're not going to help LGBT+ young people feel able to be themselves, who will?

So do young people today really need their teachers to tell them it's ok to be LGBT+? Society's views towards LGBT+ people are not set in stone. Just because we can now get married doesn't mean that the fight for our rights is over, nor does it mean that young LGBT+ people feel valued and seen in their local communities. We've come such a long way in terms of equal rights for LGBT+ people, but these could be just as quickly eroded. A picture of a lesbian couple on a London bus with bloodied faces was a reminder that the most accepting city in the world still has a long way to go. Across the Atlantic, a gunman shooting 49 people dead in a gay bar in Orlando highlighted our vulnerability, even in our so-called safe spaces.

It seems strange that I write about a cupboard helping myself and other queer students feel able to be themselves, when we often talk about 'coming out of the closet' as a form of liberation. But I guess we all just needed a safe space to be ourselves, even if that was a sweaty cupboard. Without the positivity my English showed towards LGBT+ people, I would still be battling my own internalised shame of being a gay man. The scars of being bullied and living in a society that still questions my community's worth will live with me for the rest of my life. Yet alongside them, I also carry a sense of pride. The greatest gift any teacher can give their student is the ability to believe in themselves and their abilities, irrespective of their gender identity and sexuality. It is thanks to my English teacher that I'm writing this ... You could be the next teacher to offer such a gift.

## Big gay notes from the editor

*This is the second of three chapters exploring what it is like to be an LGBT+ student taught by an LGBT+ teacher. Meeting this teacher was a turning point in Hadley Stewart's life; being able to identify with them fuelled his love for writing and the English language. He has since gone from strength to strength to be a successful writer.*

*Things are changing in many schools, but too slowly. Hadley speaks from lived experience and his view supports ours at LGBTed: that it would have been better for him and other LGBT+ students if they had more visible role models. In the opening chapter, I referred to the Stonewall School Report 2017. Hadley was yet another example of a young person who would hear the word 'gay' being used on a daily basis, often to mean something rubbish. Many schools lack 'safe spaces' for LGBT+ students, and it's a lovely idea that some students claimed a classroom, one that was barely more than a cupboard, as their safe space because their LGBT+ teacher made them feel safe there. Ask yourself: what are you doing in your school to make it safe space for LGBT+ young people? The whole school should feel safe for them. If it doesn't, are you having those difficult conversations to find out why? You may not like the answers, but this is how we can affect real change.*

*Society as a whole still does not feel safe for LGBT+ people, and there have been many sobering events in recent years that threaten us. Hadley writes about how Madonna often set the tone for what the rest of society should be doing when it comes to fighting for the LGBT+ community, and he viewed his English teacher in this way too. As he says, you could be the next teacher to offer such a gift.*

# 16 I want the world to know
*Alison Riley*

*Alison Riley has worked in education for almost two decades from primary through to secondary and further education. She has taught subjects as diverse as performing arts and computer science and everything in between. She currently works in a pastoral capacity supporting learners with maths anxiety and well-being needs, and also as Head of Dance at a theatre school. She is proud to be a visible lesbian, gay, bisexual, trans and others (LGBT+) teacher.*

As soon as I entered into my first serious same-sex relationship, I knew that I wanted to be an 'out' teacher. The question was, when would be the right time to 'come out' to my colleagues and pupils? I'd already crossed the hurdle of telling my family (completely supportive) and selective friends (all thrilled to bits), but I just couldn't seem to find the right time to let my pupils know. I'd spoken to friends about what I should do but more often than not the response was 'why bother?' or 'it is your private life, keep it private'. But although I wasn't lying, it felt like I was living a lie, every time conversations turned to family or partners; I deflected the questions or changed the subject altogether. The longer it went on, the more difficult it became for me to drop it into conversation.

In my small town, it is common that 'gay', 'lesbian' and 'homo' are perfectly acceptable insults for everything from your mate to your enemy or even your broken computer/car/phone can be accused of being 'gay'. In other words, weird, broken, wrong.

Around the school I often heard pupils calling each other homophobic names, and even the staff used gay as an insult in shared areas. The culture of the school was that gay was wrong and something to be mocked.

One day I overheard a colleague on the phone to a parent whose teenager had come out as gay, and the parent was less than happy from the sound of things. The teacher assured the parent that it was a phase and she was sure he would grow out of it. I was horrified by the ignorance and decided that at the next opportunity I would tell them about my partner. The next day, in the staffroom, the conversation turned to sexuality and labels. I felt my face flush and took a deep breath and announced to the room that I used to identify as bisexual, but I should probably say I am pansexual as sex and gender don't dictate who I fall in love with. Most staff looked on with interest, but one teacher laughed out loud and declared 'one day you'll make your mind up, I call it greedy'. I tried to explain that it didn't mean all at the same time, but they were too impressed with their wit that my protests fell on deaf ears and my confidence was well and truly knocked. I went home that night and discussed the day with my partner, and I felt like a real failure. I'd finally come out to my colleagues, but it felt jaded by the reaction of that teacher. It had been so difficult to come out to my colleagues, but I did feel lighter, like I had taken a step toward something positive and bright.

The next day I was called to cover a Personal Social and Health Education lesson about bullying. I began the first activity by giving each group a scenario to find a solution for, but within the first few minutes of the lesson the boys were calling each other 'gays'. I stopped the lesson and asked the class to stop their work and face the board. I drew a face on the board and asked the class to describe someone they admired, and the words came thick and fast: strong, kind, happy, helpful, smart, intelligent, generous and on. I then drew another face and asked then to describe someone they didn't like and again the words came out in a tumble: stupid, ugly, thick, rude, nasty and gay. *Gay.* I asked them why they had chosen those words and we went through each one in turn; it was a fantastic discussion until we got to the word gay, and no one could tell me why they used the word gay as an insult. I asked them which of the words they would use to describe me and, thankfully, they all used the positive ones – I had a great relationship with this class – but I replied, 'you missed one'. They responded with confusion, so I said 'gay, I am gay'.

I realised that if it was difficult for me, an adult in a secure relationship with supportive friends and family to come out, then how much more difficult would it be for a young person who is still finding their way in the world. I had a responsibility, a duty to these pupils to be a positive role model, living proof that you can be successful, out and proud.

The following break something wonderful happened: a pupil who had been quiet and withdrawn sought me out to tell me that they were gay, and when I came out to the class, it gave him confidence to do the same. The next day another pupil told me they were bi, and that afternoon, Alice requested that I call her Dean and use the pronoun 'he'. Word had travelled fast and in the staffroom the gender/sexuality conversation continued, but this time with an air of positive curiosity and intention to learn.

Over the past 18 months, I have worked as a supply teacher in many schools. I always wear my LGBT+ badge on my lanyard and 'come out' at the first appropriate opportunity. It may well be my personal life, but if I personally show support and acceptance of all pupils in my classes, I validate them and show them that they are not alone.

Since coming out to that class, a parent contacted me directly to thank me for teaching her son about LGBT+ and to be accepting of others. She said that he made a new friend at school that was 'gay, just like Miss Riley, and that's kinda cool'.

## Big gay notes from the editor

*This chapter highlights how being visible and authentic as an LGBT+ teacher can help students to modify their language, such as the use of the word 'gay' as meaning something 'rubbish'. This in turn reduces the amount of homophobic language and homophobic bullying amongst our young people. Often, once it becomes clear they know an LGBT+ person and there is in fact one in the room, it makes the issue more tangible to them. I have lost count of how many times I have heard a student say 'but I don't know any gay people'. Cue jazz hands from me.*

*Alison also writes how one comment about sexuality from a colleague had a negative impact on her. As leaders, ask yourself if you have these people on your staff body and how you would respond if you heard these comments yourself or you had received a complaint from somebody else. As teachers, ask yourself if you are still seeking to learn every day – as you should be – to become better. A lot of what passes for 'banter' in the classroom and the staff room can be deeply toxic.*

# 17 The best you can be is yourself
*Zoe Defoe*

*Zoe Defoe started teaching at age 19 in French after school and weekend clubs whilst studying at university. Before training as a teacher, she worked in France in different employment sectors including a stint at Disneyland Paris. She was recently diagnosed with Addison's disease (part of APS type 2, something JFK also had), and this made her take stock of many things. She is now embracing single life and pursuing her own personal dreams and passions.*

The thing with love is that it always follows an unexpected path. You are taken down roads you never foresaw, up mountains you never expected to climb and into cavernous depths of emotion you never knew you had. My journey starts in 1979, the year I was born. The year that Margaret Thatcher came to power, everyone was on strike and… a nudist beach was opened in Brighton… My parents, staunchly Tory and followers of the Church of England, were blissfully unaware of the future of their first born daughter.

In 1987 I moved schools, having been bullied by a brute of a female headteacher at my first primary school, my parents put me into a small private school with a view to improving my education. It served me well, and all my interests and passions stem from this time. In 1988 the Education Reform Act came to being and the National Curriculum was born. Thankfully given the experiences in my previous school, this was the year that corporal punishment in schools was also banned. It was not a good year for love though, Section 28 was brought in citing that one must not "promote the teaching in any maintained school of the acceptability of homosexuality as a pretend family relationship." It is probably because of this that I remained completely unaware of the possibility of anything but male and female couples.

Looking back there were signs, I just had no idea at the time. I remember standing in an assembly once, next to a girl who was slightly taller than me, confident, with short brown hair and blue eyes. I seemed drawn to her and kept looking at her features. She had pierced ears too I noticed. I was just shy of my tenth birthday, and I told my mum that I wanted to have my hair cut short and my ears pierced. So off I went to the hairdressers. The hairdresser tied my hair into a ponytail and chopped it off. Gone. Then I got my ears pierced. So complete with new look I returned to school the next week and was completely oblivious as to the symbolism of what I had just done.

I was definitely a naive child, unworldly, not very streetwise, unaware of the bigger world – much preferring to bury myself in books, nature and art. So when I joined secondary school, it was all a big wake-up call. Very early on, I started to get a lot of attention from boys. I was asked out in the first week by a boy two years older than me who unbeknown to me all the other girls wanted – actor, gymnast, always lead in school plays, etc. I ran away from him, too shy and clueless to know what to do. Sadly my dealings with boys thereafter weren't great – I was sexually and physically assaulted by several in my time there – I was hit with all sorts, groped in various places, and then there was general bullying from whoever – male or female – was on the bandwagon at that time. Then one day the school caretaker followed me into the toilets and opened the cubicle door from the outside. There I was at my most vulnerable, this huge man filling the doorway and me wondering how on earth to get out. I looked towards the main door as if I had heard something and it was enough for him to make a hasty retreat. Thank goodness. I had to sit and watch him being praised and given presents upon his leaving the school and desperately wanted to stand up and expose him for who he was. Stupidly, I never reported it. Who would believe me…?

"She's a lesbian!" "She is look at her, the way she's leaning on her friend there." This was the first time I'd heard the word. "What's a lesbian?" No one would tell me. I remained clueless. However, from the ages of 13 to 16, I had a clandestine relationship with the most popular boy in our year. I never really felt or was aware that I was missing that zing. I think I always wanted affection and love, even if it was in all the wrong places. He showed me attention (albeit when no one else was around) and I genuinely really liked him at the time.

"You never really understand a person until you consider things from his point of view… until you climb into his skin and walk around in it." My English teacher was reading the part of Atticus Finch in To Kill a Mockingbird by Harper Lee and I was gazing out of the window. "Zöe, what do you think this means?" I snapped back awake at the sound of the soft Northern Irish accent calling my name, and this wave flashed through me. I was 15 and had never felt anything like this before. Yet every time I was in that room, I felt the same. I studied her wave of auburn hair and blue eyes, willingly hanging on every word. She was my first lesbian crush. I do wonder if she even knew or ever suspected.

I kept this new realisation to myself, and it would remain this way until I started university when I was 19. I made a friend on the first day there, but, as an evangelical christian, the moment she found out I might be gay she dropped me like a hat. She said, "I can love a gay person but God says it's wrong." I didn't find her actions particularly loving though. I still didn't fully know myself at this point – I knew I had these feelings, I didn't fully understand them though and I desperately wanted to talk to someone about how I was feeling.

It would be another two years until I had the courage or the opportunity. I was 21 and working in B&Q every weekend (one of three jobs I had) to earn money to pay my way through university. I was sitting in the staff canteen one lunchtime chatting to two of my colleagues, and the lady just came out with it, "my daughter is gay and I love her very much." I was internally processing this and said nothing at the time. A couple of days later I went and spoke to her and said, "I think I might be like you daughter." She said, "look let me have a word with her, it may help you to have a chat." She showed me a photo and I found the picture quite striking – it was a small, square, sepia picture. She was quite boyish to look at with a feminine toothy smile but somehow familiar to me (all the women who I would come to have on my path have been recognisable somehow). Jo agreed to chat with me and we spent every day chatting on the phone. We got on well and eventually it was decided that I would take the train up to Manchester to meet up with her. She met me at the train station and took me to her car and we drove through Manchester, her chain smoking along the way, past the

Man Utd stadium where I got a load of free packets of tic tacs much to my joy and off to a bar for a drink and a chat. Later that evening we went to Canal Street. My first experience of the gay scene was a young lad running alongside the canal with a pair of pants on his head and everyone around us laughing! We walked in to the Via Fosse and carried on our evening. Two guys on the opposite table asked if we were in love and that they were like it once. We had only just met and I was just one massive ball of nerves, anxiety and excitement. We looked at each other and I went in for a kiss. It was my first kiss with a woman and I was trying to digest how it felt. It felt soft and it was nice and it didn't feel at all wrong. I suddenly felt like my head was in the clouds and I couldn't think straight. What did this all mean…?

I returned home the next day and she made clear that there would not be any more beyond that kiss. I was fine with that – I was finally starting to realise who I was. I went back to university and continued to wrestle with my feelings. I then made the momentous decision to tell my mum. I got home from university and told her that there was something I needed to tell her. She could tell I was upset and followed me upstairs. "What is it?" She said. "Have you quit uni?"

"No worse than that." I couldn't get the words out through tears. "I think I might be gay."

A look of surprise crossed her face. I had not thought things through nor anticipated or prepared for any type of response. "It's probably just a phase if you come back when you're 40 I might believe you." This was not, for whatever reason, the response I wanted, so through tears I wrote her a letter explaining that I have felt like this for years and that it's not a phase and that I just know, etc. My phraseology perhaps hadn't helped me here. I then got out of the house and walked down by the river, my sanctuary, just to clear my head. When I got home mum had written a small note saying, "you are what you are, why do you expect a big debate about everything." We didn't talk much about it after that but I did ask whether to tell my dad and she said not to.

I told my three sisters who just told me that they loved me and that they had kind of suspected. Then I told my friends. The last person I told was my best friend, and I don't know why but I felt that she would be the hardest person to tell and was just blown away by her wonderful reaction to me telling her. It made no difference – 14 years of friendship was safe, I had done the hard part now, all those that mattered knew. I joined the LGBT+ society at university which had just been set up by a guy called Chris who always texted "cool" as "kewl" and was introduced to other like-minded people. We then started going to a local pub which was always shrouded in mystery and now I understood why. This was the first time I saw lots of gay couples together, in the smoky, dark, Army and Navy pub in Chelmsford. Jo had come back to Essex from Manchester and I had made a new friend, Loic, whilst teaching English to French students. I was open about myself which gave him the freedom to discover himself. I introduced him to Jo and my social life was ignited. The men at the pub would always comment on how well I moved my body on the dance floor and I would get them joining in with me and having a giggle. My confidence in who I was, was growing.

Then a new venue, Chicagos, opened up with a Sunday evening gay night, and we would regularly go down there. It was there one night that Peter, now Phoenix (or Cilla as we called him), introduced me to Laura. We started dancing together and she ran her hands across my stomach and asked to kiss me. I felt a tingle. I didn't fancy her and was too shy to do anything; anyway she gave me her number and we agreed to meet the next day. We met up and I still didn't fancy her but went with the flow. We kissed and it was lovely. I was definitely gay. This was someone who knew what she wanted, but I wasn't really attracted to her. I think the newness of it, and the desire to find me (I was more than ready at this point being 24) swept me along. She was the first person I slept with and in every way was totally wrong for me. She slept around, if I wasn't in her bed, another man or woman was, she was addicted to everything and just really not my kind of person. After spending three hours on trains to see her each time to find that she had love bites from other people on her neck/body, I was not happy. I think the last straw came after I'd had a big operation, and I phoned her as soon as I got home and I just knew – I sobbed and told her enough was enough. I didn't see or speak to her again. I was out to a few select people at the school I worked at whilst in this relationship. I remember my head of department referring to another lady in the department as being a bit strange. I later found out that she had been married to a man but fell in love with and had an affair with a female headteacher. She ended it with her husband and told her two grown-up sons who were great about it. She said he was a lovely man, but she just didn't love him very much and that her only regret was that she didn't have enough time with her true love – they had only been together three years when she died. It was clear she was struggling with the loss, and I told her about myself and offered my support.

Despite the odd kiss with a few women, after Laura, I was then single for five years until I met Claire online. She messaged me first and there was no photo on her profile so I asked to see a picture and I was curious about her. We started dating and a month later I properly asked her out in the middle of our local ice rink. She was incredibly wobbly after that and needed to sit down. A week later I got my answer whilst standing on a bridge over the canal. She said she, "had nothing to lose and would give it a go." At that moment a load of fireworks went up opposite us, it was a few days before Bonfire Night. The people in my department at the new school I was working at knew I had a girlfriend and in a way it made it easier for me to be out than if I had been single. We were together for nearly two years. We met each other's parents, she was at my 30th birthday, and my dad knew by then and was fine with it. Claire and I had relatively little in common – I was outdoorsy, whereas she preferred to be at home socialising via her computer on World of Warcraft. We could both talk for England however. She was head over heels in love with her best friend, and our relationship was never destined to last. We eventually called it a day and remained friends for another six years after.

A few months after breaking up with Claire, I had heard about a staff band at work so thought I would find out more and was introduced to Lucy the lead singer. She was bold, confident, overtly sexual and not afraid to speak her mind. She suggested I come along. The first time I saw her properly was on the school stage singing. She seemed so familiar to me, like I'd always known her. She owned it and I was mesmerised. It felt like she was singing to me. That evening her, I and the other lead singer were in the car and she referred to her lesbian past. I was even more intrigued now. A married woman with two kids, what did she mean. Much like my first experience, a day or so later I told her about myself. We got talking and she said that she was unhappy in her marriage and just wanted him to love her and show her affection, but he seemed unable to. I instantly didn't like him – he was 22 years older than her, had been her teacher and in her words, "wore her down," i.e. groomed her. He was slimy, creepy and ugly – I had no idea what someone so pretty was doing with "him". As time went on, she said that she wanted someone that was the complete opposite to him and it became clear that I was it. I took her for a walk along the river, our hands met each other's and I gently tugged at her hand to bring her into me. The kiss went on for a lot longer than I expected, and I could see afterwards that she was struck by this whole wave of emotions. She told me later that if the kiss hadn't have been so good, we wouldn't have carried on. A week or so later she took me to a music room at the school, guitar in hand and sang, "taking chances" just for me. Probably at that point the most romantic thing anyone had done for me. We had loads in common and would spend our days outside playing the guitar, doing art, sending each other messages in French, doing Zumba and intellectualising about a whole myriad of subjects. In essence we had a great friendship with the odd sneaky bit of romance. I did start to wonder if she just really wasn't in to women in the same way, but I think I was just too much for her – she said she couldn't deal with someone more emotional than herself. She now identifies as pansexual and is still with the man she eventually left her husband for.

A few months after Lucy and I split, I met Jen online. I kept being drawn back to her profile picture, time and time again, and in the end gave up and messaged her. She was training to be in the Royal Air Force and was super fit and cheeky. We met under the clock at Waterloo Station for our first date and did a tour of the Tate Modern, walked along the banks of the Thames and paused to kiss under a bridge near to the houses of parliament. She kissed the way I kissed and wanted to be kissed. We had a lovely day with a boat ride on the Thames as the highlight. We looked very much in love and people smiled at us everywhere we went. As we kissed goodbye at a station saying that the next time we would meet would be in Exeter, where she lived, we didn't expect to both get lost in the underground and end up on the same platform again… Jen and I had that spark and we certainly had a very passionate relationship, but it soon became clear that she didn't have the commitment and after a beautiful holiday in the Lake District, she called it a day; Jen choosing at that point to completely cut communication with me as she felt it was the best way to move on, leaving me without real answers or closure. I was still working at the same school where Lucy and I worked and was now in a different department. I talked about my relationships as everyone else did until one day I got called into a meeting with my head of department. "We would rather you didn't talk about your relationships with other members of staff." Somebody had said something. "But everyone else talks about their relationships, their husbands and boyfriends, etc." She had no answer to that. A year later, the Equality Act 2010 was introduced and that conversation wouldn't have been allowed.

However, in 2014, I started working at a school which I began to feel at home in. I loved it, had begun to make friends and had begun to share with some of those friends that I was gay. One of them I remember said, "I'm a little surprised but it doesn't change anything." I guess unlike my unkempt youth, I had started to embrace my feminity and "looked less gay." In the first couple of years there I'd had several dates but didn't find anyone I'd liked enough to want to pursue it any further, despite a few of their best efforts. My sister said she always admired the fact that I always waited for the right person. I think it's true that love often comes along when you least expect it, and you'll know at the time whether you want to pursue it.

It was 2016, a new group of teachers started the school and I remember a group of them coming into the English as an Additional Language (EAL) classroom for training and being immediately struck by one lady in particular who I smiled at. However, she didn't respond much at the time and I put this down to being new and nerves. We found that we had evening duty on the same night so we started chatting over dinner on those evenings. One night we got talking about a student who was openly gay. I said, "I know what it's like because I'm gay." She then turned round and said, "so am I." My jaw dropped. This high heel wearing, made up, power dressed woman, with two kids and an ex-husband is gay?! I didn't say much after that but sent her an email to her work address saying something to the effect that "it's always nice to have like-minded friends and here's my number." We started texting and agreed to go to the cinema one evening – except I had to keep blowing her out…

Unbeknown to me I was very sick. I had this lingering cough for months and then had the most horrendous cold for six weeks which wouldn't shift and then one day after evening duty I began to feel very unwell. I had gone home and was in bed for a few days when spots appeared on my upper thigh which turned out to be shingles. (We later found out that I had Addison's disease which was why I was so ill all the time.) Lou, not to be put off by my blowing her out for the umpteenth time, sent me a bouquet of flowers with the words, "get well soon, tu me manques." At which point I was sold. It was some time before I got to see her at her house and despite feeling terrible, I instantly felt relaxed and safe with her. Both somewhat nervous, we shared our first kiss. This enigmatic, older woman – I couldn't believe my luck!

I don't think either of us realised the impact that we would have as a couple on the school community. Our relationship grew, everyone in the workplace knew about us and we had to make a decision about whether we were out to the students too. We decided that our first "outing" as a couple would be the sixth form leaver's ball. Students and parents were there and students asked us if we were together and we were honest with them. We proudly presented a certain young man with a cupid badge as it was because we had been discussing him that we found out about each other. He was absolutely over the moon and gave us both a massive hug. The evening went well and we relaxed into the atmosphere and could just be ourselves.

Several months later, we did something which I could never have envisaged ever happening growing up. Staff were asked whether they would be interested in supporting the rainbow laces campaign. I was 100% up for this and told the organiser that I would like to do something. She suggested introducing the campaign to the students. I was thinking, "fantastic", and thought I would run it by Lou and see whether she would do it with me. Naturally she was nervous about the idea and thought it only right to ask her boys as they were students at the school whether they would mind. They were totally supportive. So we got up on the stage, two openly out, respected members of staff, a couple, standing in the school chapel, launching the rainbow laces campaign. It was groundbreaking. We showed a video timeline of various moments in LGBT+ history and referred to how things were different when we were younger, and we inferred without explicitly saying it that we were gay and a couple. We didn't need to shout it from the rooftops. We needed to normalise it. What surprised us was the absolute non-reaction. We were two respected staff members before they knew, and we remained that way afterwards. We were in a school where LGBT+ staff and students were supported and where respect and open-mindedness were valued. Staff and student well-being were central to everything. It made me look and reflect upon just how far we've come.

Change really is possible if we're willing to be that change. If we love and accept ourselves, we allow others to do the same. Whatever our own individual journeys, we all bring something to the table, and we all have experiences which can be drawn upon to help others. We can show the world that love is love and that it's something to be immensely proud of.

## Big gay notes from the editor

*In this chapter, Zoe bravely shares some genuinely traumatic experiences in order to show the extent your school years shape your identity and path in life. We have seen many teachers that are fearful of being visible and authentic LGBT+ role models due to their own experiences at school. Zoe talked about her own relationships in the staffroom, just as everyone else did, but was told by her head of department that they would rather she didn't. Many of us can empathise with this and would feel it very deeply, but it is important to know that as LGBT+ teachers we are now protected by the Equality Act 2010.[1] The "protected characteristics" in the Act are age, disability, gender reassignment, race, religion or belief, sex, sexual orientation, marriage and civil partnership, and pregnancy and maternity. Section 149 of the Equality Act 2010 states:*

*Schools are subject to the equality duty and must, in the exercise of their functions, have due regard to the need to*

- *Eliminate unlawful discrimination, harassment and victimisation and other conduct prohibited by the Act.*
- *Advance equality of opportunity between people who share a protected characteristic and those who do not.*
- *Foster good relations between people who share a protected characteristic and those who do not.*

*This means teachers and school leaders have a duty to support their LGBT+ colleagues. Are you aware of this Act in your school? What are you doing as a teacher or a leader to support your colleagues?*

*This chapter reflects on how important it is, and how great it feels as an LGBT+ person, to finally find the right school to work in, where you feel safe and supported. During a teacher retention crisis, it is a sad state of affairs that a vast number of teachers in our network have not felt empowered to be authentic at work. Not all teachers are a fit for all schools, of course, for a variety of reasons, but when this is due to a protected characteristic – and has no impact on one's ability to perform effectively in the role – this is totally unacceptable. When a teacher feels they are in the right school, they are more motivated and more likely to make a significant, vocal contribution to the school community because doing so doesn't undermine their safety.*

*As Zoe writes, "change really is possible if we're willing to be that change. If we love and accept ourselves, we allow others to do the same." This change starts in our schools.*

## Note

1 http://www.legislation.gov.uk/ukpga/2010/15/contents

# 18 You've gotta give 'em hope
*Michael Williams*

*Michael Williams has been Assistant Principal at a Church of England middle school in Redditch, Worcestershire, for the past four years. In this chapter he writes about how he, as an experienced school leader, believes in values-led leadership.*

"You've gotta give 'em hope." Harvey Milk spoke these immortal words in unapologetic, loud and proud defiance against a proposition which sought to ban gay teachers working in schools. Proposition Six, led by California state politician John Briggs and religious anti-gay rights activist Anita Bryant, was to ban any discussion – positive or negative – of lesbian, gay, bisexual, trans and others (LGBT+) people in schools and forbid gay teachers from working in education.

When I took a position as Assistant Principal at a Church of England faith school, I had never imagined this school would be the place where I would feel the most accepted as an openly gay man. I was raised on a council estate in Redditch – a new town on the outskirts of Birmingham. My education too was coloured by the mire of Section 28. The one time gay people were mentioned during my time in school was a sex education lesson at age 16, where I was told that gay people were more likely to be HIV+ and had sex in public toilets. I had never met a gay person, other than one boy who came out in a geography lesson at high school, and was pelted with stones as he left school that day. He never came back. All I wanted was to escape – escape the community, escape the intolerance, escape the hate. In my wildest dreams, I had never imagined that I would be returning to the same school a decade later as an openly gay teacher.

As I stepped over the threshold on my first day, so many memories came flooding back: copying passages from a yellowed, dog-eared copy of the Good News Bible, the dire trudge to the assembly hall for another dreary chorus of *Amazing Grace*, the time my IT teacher asked the class, "So, which of you is going to grow up to be a gay boy?" My stomach was knotted with anxiety. This could have been the biggest mistake of my life. I had been openly gay for seven years, ever since leaving Redditch for university; I had promised myself when I left that I would never be in the closet again. I had managed this on every front, except for in school. Though I had always been open with other teachers, when it came to pupils my interactions were punctuated with pregnant pauses, careful omissions and the art of changing the subject any time I thought the dreaded question might have been looming.

I had promised myself; this time would be different.

I had imagined the moment a thousand times. As a senior leader, I was used to public speaking, delivering assemblies and conveying messages clearly – but this time, I was a terrified 13-year-old again, coming out to a friend for the first time, terrified that I would be laughed at and rejected. I had planned my message with military precision – I was telling the story of Harvey Milk and how the pride of one man had helped to spread the message of pride around the world. Three hundred eyes were leering at me, pupils and staff. Short of running for the door and feigning a sudden illness, there was no way out.

"This is why I'm proud every day to be gay." I was forensically scanning the crowd, searching for wry smiles and gasps of horror. I clock a couple of pupils throwing each other looks of confusion, another gazing vacantly at the ceiling tiles. Then I spot the one reaction I hadn't anticipated. Why it hadn't occurred to me before, I have no idea, but there he was, a little boy, with the broadest smile across his face, staring directly back at me. Immediately, I was transported back to when I was sat in his place – this same assembly hall, where I had spent so many mornings sat cross-legged on the cold, wooden floor, silently screaming out to hear a story with some relevance to my life. I flashed a smile back to him – my younger self – and carried on.

By the time I was back at my desk, my inbox was inundated with messages of support from staff. By the end of break time, two pupils had come out to me, and another had come to let me know he was "cool with it." By the end of the week, a group of pupils had come to tell me they wanted to form a "Pride Group" and support other pupils identifying as LGBT+. I couldn't quite believe it.

It wasn't always as easy. There were times I walked past a conversation at break time, and it would suddenly become hushed, punctuated by cutting, surreptitious glares across the quad. There was the pupil who told me, "My mum said you shouldn't talk about that sort of thing in school." There was the group of pupils from a neighbouring high school who had heard about what happened and decided to wait for me on the gate at the end of the day in order to see whether I was going to be bold enough to show up to duty and stand defiantly next to them. But this was different now – I wasn't just doing this for me, I was doing this for every LGBT+ pupil in our school, every ally, and every time I had pretended not to hear or see the abuse in the past. This was about being strong for them – courage and conviction to create change. I had been a part of this community where I had felt hopeless – and I was committed to being a part of seeing that change.

Over the next few weeks, I found myself asking "Why here?" Of all the schools I had worked in, why is it the faith school on the council estate where I felt most comfortable being me? Naturally, I had presumed that I would meet the same obtuse, homophobic views I had encountered when I was a pupil at the school, whether rooted in archaic interpretation of scripture, or the insular small mindedness which I remember so well from my life on the neighbouring council estate. It was bewildering – it shouldn't have been that easy.

Over time, I have come to realise why our school is so special. At its heart, our school is about values – nurturing the qualities of character which encourage our community to lead happy and meaningful lives. Whether these values are rooted in teachings from the Bible, in our commitment to the arts or in our shared belief that education should be about celebration of diversity and individuality, it is this which makes our school distinctive. Our leadership team – made up of five women and a gay man – roots every decision, every initiative and every conversation in a deep sense of this core purpose.

Values-led leadership is about creating and sustaining a culture which is grounded in understanding, compassion and shared purpose. It's about understanding the role you play in the community and what your community needs from you. It's about not being afraid to use the word "love." This culture permeates everything – every lesson, every assembly, every experience, every interaction comes back to these values. When we hold ourselves to account around these fundamental values, we grow a culture which perpetuates them, from our teachers, to our lunchtime supervisors and administrators, to our pupils themselves.

Four months later, we had pupils identifying as gay, bisexual and pansexual, we had trans pupils and we had pupils respecting each other's choice of pronouns and expression of their own gender identity – the culture was shifting. I knew that there was more I could do. I shared my story.

On a grey, miserable Tuesday afternoon in February, a tired, shivering staff made their way into a Continuing Professional Development (CPD) session. They were expecting me to spend the next hour talking about differentiation and support for children with dyslexia, so, perhaps understandably, most had taken their seats and then glazed over in anticipation of whether I would finish early. Over the next hour, I opened up in a way I never would have thought possible. I started with a picture of me in my uniform from my days as a pupil at the school – cue cutesy reactions from teachers slowly recognising this isn't the session they had expected. I shared the good times and the bad: I shared what it felt like to realise I was gay and go through years of shame, and terrified that I would be "found out"; I shared the times I self-harmed and wished anything that I could be like everybody else; I shared the moments in school where I was made to feel like I didn't belong, where the only time I was hearing the word "gay" was when shouted at me down a corridor between lessons as I scurried away and pretended I hadn't heard it. This was the proudest moment of my career.

I shared the difference it would have made to have had visibility – to have been seen and felt like I belonged. For me, an inclusive school starts with visibility and unapologetic, unwavering celebration. When we normalise visibility around LGBT+ culture, we create an environment in which LGBT+ people can feel that they belong; whether it be the classroom where the story we are reading includes two mums and their daughter or solving the maths equation about how many eggs are needed to bake a cake for Billy's two uncles' wedding, by representing diversity in our classrooms, we foster a value much deeper than just tolerance and respect. We develop understanding, appreciation and celebration. We challenge and confront prejudice in all its forms. We grow a culture in which there are no outsiders.

Two weeks after this, I had a conversation with a colleague in a freezing, gloomy office. He had just come out to a pupil as gay, as a part of supporting the pupil with understanding their own sexuality. He was the first pupil he had ever told. My heart swelled to see how proud he was and to know the difference it must have made to that young person to feel seen and understood. It made me recognise how, as gay teachers, it's just as important for us to feel seen, to feel that we belong, to feel proud. Too often, I speak with colleagues in other schools who say they feel they can't share their sexuality in work – some schools where homophobia runs rife and goes unpunished, others where the age-old mantra "what you do in your bedroom is no business of mine" still rings true. For me, being an openly gay teacher is not just about the visibility it creates for pupils: this is who I am, and I am unapologetically, unquestionably loud and proud of it. This is about me valuing myself.

Speaking on 25th June 1978, Harvey Milk said, "Like every other group, we must be judged by our leaders and by those who are themselves gay, those who are visible. For invisible, we remain in limbo – a myth." For the first 18 years of my life, LGBT+ people were just this: a myth. Now, my school is a place where all aspects of LGBT+ culture are embraced and celebrated within our school community. Just this week, a pupil ran up to me at break time to tell me, "Guess what, Sir? I've just told my friends I'm bisexual." Behind her stood her friends, smiling and cheering. Moments like that are exactly why I work in education. The world is not always a welcoming place for LGBT+ people, but, for her, in that moment, she was accepted, valued and celebrated. As long as our school community can be a place of hope for young LGBT+ people, I will be immeasurably proud of everyone and everything that makes it so special.

## Big gay notes from the editor

*Harvey Milk embodied values-led leadership, which Michael suggests is about creating and sustaining a culture that is grounded in understanding, compassion and shared purpose. It's about understanding the role you play in the community and what your community needs from you. It can be in a speech in an assembly, and it can be "in the classroom, where the story we are reading includes two mums and their daughter or solving the maths equation about how many eggs are needed to bake a cake for Billy's two uncles' wedding." Values-led leadership is aspiring to embody more than just "tolerance and respect": it is celebrating.*

*This seems like a good opportunity to mention Hannah Wilson, who is a huge inspiration to me and was a catalyst to the creation of LGBTed. Hannah is a former executive headteacher of two schools and an independent consultant who specialises in leadership development and training. She is also the co-founder of #WomenEd and the founder of #DiverseEd. A key takeaway for teachers for this chapter would be to further explore the idea of values-led leadership, of which she is a pioneer, on her website.[1] Do you consider yourself to be a values-led leader?*

*"All I wanted was to escape – escape the community, escape the intolerance, escape the hate." Michael's story of his experiences in his school days resonates so much with me. I remember the only gay person I knew – my best friend at the time – was treated even worse than I was because he was "out." I knew I was different, but I didn't know I was gay because I didn't recognise any shared characteristics with him. But in hindsight, I believe the fact we had that unspoken common ground explained why we got on so well. That and a mutual love of ABBA. I was particularly moved by Michael's account of the young boy who smiled in the assembly when he realised his teacher was gay. I'm sure we all wish to have had that moment at some point in our school days, a moment that is both gently reassuring and life-affirming.*

*As Michael says, we are not doing this for ourselves. We are doing it for every LGBT+ student in the school, every ally, and for every time we had pretended not to hear or see the abuse in the past. By being a successful, confident "out" teacher, you are showing these young people that they are OK. You are giving them hope.*

## Note

1 www.hannah-wilson.co.uk

# 19 The invisible girl
*Jennifer Heaton*

*Jennifer Heaton is a writer and film critic based in Glasgow. An alumnus of the London Film School, Jennifer writes for film, television and stage in various genres, but always with a feminist viewpoint and intersectional inclusion. She has written for her website Alternative Lens since 2012 reviewing the latest film releases, alongside a monthly opinion piece for In Their Own League, and is a featured critic on Rotten Tomatoes and CherryPicks.*

Growing up in the 1990s and 1900s, you didn't learn about gay people from your teachers or parents. You learnt about them through playground insults. The unwillingness to start an honest conversation about sexuality in schools only allowed the cycle of ignorance to continue. All we had were the words of the school bullies and, according to them, being gay was equitable to being a child abuser. Rarely a day in the schoolyard went by without words like "poofter" or "bum boy" being thrown around in a casually disparaging way. Many of those jibes were directed at me.

I wasn't exactly an overtly feminine child, but I was extremely sensitive and a far cry from the other (presumably) cis-hetero boys. It was less an abundance of femininity but more my lack of masculinity; at least not any I didn't put on in vain attempts to fit in. I first experienced homophobic abuse at age nine just for being perceived as gay. I was made to believe there was something inherently wrong with me and, because no adults could say anything otherwise, I believed that I deserved it.

If the poor awareness of gay people back then was damaging, the absolute silence about the transgender community was deafening. I remember first learning the term from a television documentary I found whilst channel surfing late one night. It immediately fascinated me in a way I couldn't understand, but even then I knew it wasn't a life you should aspire to. I still vividly recall watching this child recount the abuse he and his trans mother received because of her gender identity, and it struck a chord I never knew I had. I quickly learnt to bury that chord.

After my primary school years were up, my parents decided to send me to boarding school; they believed I wasn't getting enough attention in state education. My new school was and still is seen as one of the best in the country, though its atmosphere was far less welcoming at the time. It was the kind of institution that only saw you as worthwhile if you were an academic genius or an Olympic-level athlete; at least that's the impression many staff encouraged. As an overweight, academically disinclined, anxiety-ridden, closeted trans kid, I was far from that ideal.

The mild playtime bullying of my youth intensified to a fevered pitch, and as I was boarding I was now trapped 24/7 with my abusers. I often couldn't even sleep without fear of something awful happening to me. The homophobic taunts carried over, and with puberty on the rise it only grew more intense. I was something of a late bloomer, and the lack of progress on my journey to masculinity gave the bullies a new source of mockery. I found myself begging for puberty to hurry up, thinking it would finally "fix" me. Eventually it did come, but it only worsened my dysphoria; not that I even knew to call it that.

My mental health began to take a deep dive. I was sent to see an educational psychologist, where I was misdiagnosed with dyscalculia as reasoning for my academic struggles. My attempts to seek help from my housemaster were mostly met with indifference, and the onus was instead put on me to "man up" and accept it was just "lads' banter". This only led to further mistrust of the staff and shamed me into not reporting some of the more severe incidents, some of which, in retrospect, I'd class as sexual abuse. I even made a vain attempt at suicide on school grounds, attempting to asphyxiate myself with my own tie. Even that was quickly swept under the rug and forgotten about.

However, I had one bright spot beginning in my fourth form year. A new drama teacher had arrived then to take over the department, and from our first lesson with him it was clear he wasn't another member of the old boys' club. He wasn't the first (or last) openly gay teacher at our school, but Mr. C was the first that did very little to hide it. He had a larger than life personality, a perky spring in his step, and didn't seem to take life too seriously. He was the kind of teacher who'd say things in class like, "Oh, that Hamlet gets on my tits!" in the middle of class without batting an eyelid. That's not to say he was unprofessional. In the classroom, he remained a teacher first and would call you out for slacking off, but it was clear that frustration was drawn from a desire to see you succeed. He was the best kind of teacher, in that he didn't have to dilute his identity to be respected.

I was never particularly good at acting. I was so used to putting on a front to hide myself, embracing another persona proved difficult; it's hard to act when you're already putting on a performance 24/7. I mainly did drama because it was one of the few subjects that didn't demand long essays or complex maths, and it was an opportunity to escape my otherwise distressing school environment. However, I may have unknowingly let my dormant truth slip in on occasion. I particularly remember one exercise where we did scenes from *A Midsummer Night's Dream*, and for mine I took on the role of Helena. It was my first time playing a female part, and I threw myself into it. Unlike every other role, it all came naturally to me and without understanding why I actually enjoyed myself. I recall finishing my scene and the astounded reaction of my classmates and Mr. C. Where did this energy suddenly come from? How did that come out of this shy reserved child? Why was it this role the one that did it? It took me until years later to unpack all of that.

Even though I was far from a model student, Mr. C became one of the few teachers I actively trusted. Coming to his classes felt like a respite from everything I hated about my life, and his openness and generosity was so inspiring I kept up with the class right through to A Level. I fondly remember the chats we'd have before and after lessons as a class, where he'd open up a bit and speak his mind to us about current topics like peers. One of those times, Mr. C spoke to us about the actual complexity of gender identity and how it was a spectrum that anyone could identify at any point on, no matter how they were born. Hearing all of this, the chord I tried so hard to bury was struck again. Was this me? Did this validate how I subconsciously felt?

It took years after graduation for me to finally untangle my mind after the mess school left me in. I focused on nothing but my career goals, but I found little in reality that actually made me happy. I was still living in the façade I created for myself, and for the longest time I was too scared to take it off, for fear all the horrors of my past would start over again. Eventually, enough was enough. After turning 24, I finally came out as a transgender woman, and my life truly began.

After finally getting myself in order after that bombshell, I thought I'd maybe finally move past all the awful conditioning I put myself through, but the fear still hadn't quite left me. I thought about what might've happened if I had come out at school back then and what might be happening to kids like me there now. I knew I couldn't change my past, but I also knew I couldn't let that happen to anyone else ever again, no matter how many painful memories I might have to dredge up. And so, with great trepidation, I sent out an email to the one person there I trusted with my story.

An hour later, Mr. C responded. We spoke on the phone the next morning.

Eight years may have passed, but Mr. C was much the same. He was now married to his long-time partner and had adopted two children, but he was still teaching at the school and still the same man I met at age 14. He was, of course, appalled by my stories and offered his own apologies for not realising (yes, the whole Helena thing eventually came up!), but more importantly he agreed a dialogue needed to be opened.

A month or so later, I found myself in a restaurant with Mr. C. I chatted candidly about the abuse and isolation I faced, and he keenly listened to my advice whilst outlining what measures the school was already taking. The list was beyond impressive. All staff now had mandatory lesbian, gay, bisexual, trans and others (LGBT+) inclusivity training. There was a student-run equality network. Improvements had been made for access to mental health support. Supportive guidelines were now in place for trans pupils. Students even had the opportunity to represent the school at the local pride parade. My alma mater had gone from yet another institution where "gay" was still a dirty word to one of the most LGBT-friendly schools in the country.

As our meeting came to an end, the conversation moved away from school life and onto the greater issues of equality in the current climate. Mr. C asked me about the current negative press surrounding transgender rights and the flagrant lies and mischaracterisations. He talked about his own memories living through the media's gay panic in the 1980s and was alarmed that it seemed to be happening all over again. He asked what he could do to help.

In that moment, it really hit me. Here I was, a young trans girl scared into silence about my identity for so long because of a school environment unable to understand me, talking candidly with a teacher I now realized would have been there for me all along. It doesn't exactly mend my trauma, but it was still pretty damn cool. Still a little flustered, I gave him the best answer I could: keep speaking up. Remind people how these same fears and lies have been used to silence people before. Don't let history repeat itself.

Well, I don't think I said it quite as eloquently at the time, but it's what I meant nonetheless. Thank you, Mr. C. I don't think I'd be here without you.

## Big gay notes from the editor

*This is the third of three chapters exploring what it is like to be taught by an authentic LGBT+ teacher. It is a genuinely moving account of what it feels like to grow up in the wrong body, to be "the invisible girl" and not to understand it because those honest conversations aren't happening. Children seek validation from their role models; they need to see themselves in others in order to understand the world around them; they need those honest conversations to take place. Instead, mental health is suffering and children are being misdiagnosed due to a lack of understanding. Very little staff training takes place in schools around issues of gender identity and where it does it is usually voluntary. Remember in the Stonewall School Report 2017,[1] the research shows that half of trans students have attempted to take their own lives. Jennifer could easily have become one of the statistics.*

*As Jennifer says, students need teachers they can trust. She felt like her drama lessons were a "respite from everything she hated about herself", and it was in Mr. C's lessons that she began understanding who she was. She has since been back in touch with Mr. C to hear all about how her school has changed for the better. This shows we can learn a lot from our students' experiences. According to Jennifer, the best kind of teacher is one who doesn't have to dilute their identity to be respected. We need to support and encourage each other to be authentic. Would you expect a female colleague to be "less female" or a black colleague to be "less black"? Of course not!*

*If I were Mr. C, I would be honoured that a former student still looked up to me and thanked me in this way after so many years. What a wonderful impact to have! Be your students' Mr. C.*

## Note

1 https://www.stonewall.org.uk/school-report-2017

# 20 The moderately successful lesbian

*Nicola Sharp*

*Nicola Sharp, born and raised in Bedfordshire, has been a teacher since 2002 and is currently Head of Pedagogy and lesbian, gay, bisexual, trans and others (LGBT+) Champion in a Church of England middle school. She is partner to Jo and owner of a grumpy ginger cat called Tiger!*

'Good afternoon, I'm here to talk to you as a moderately successful lesbian.' And there began the most talked about INSET (teacher training) presentation in Henlow history. This was September 2018 but took a lifetime to achieve…

My story begins in a small Bedfordshire village in 1973. I was the first born daughter of ordinary working parents. Luckily my mum has never had fixed ideas of what girls should wear or how they should be so I grew up wearing trousers, having short hair, riding my bike and playing football (never for a school or a local team – this just didn't exist in the late 1970s and through the 1980s).

Lower school was a happy affair: lovely teachers, teaching what they were interested in, Pre-National Curriculum days and Mr Happs letting me attend after school footie practice. I had a close family, lots of friends and not a care in the world. Some people often remarked that I was a 'tomboy' – what an archaic word that is! – but that never mattered, I was just enjoying my childhood.

The first time, I think I noticed I was different was in early 1983 when the Eurythmics popped up on Top of the Pops. I remember looking at Annie Lennox belt out Sweet Dreams in her black suit and red tie and knew in that moment my admiration for her wasn't just innocent admiration. With no gay role models in the media, or community I lived in, let alone knowing or understanding the word lesbian, I carried on through my middle school years, but that image has always stayed with me.

Again my four years at middle school (Years 5–8 in modern money) were some of my happiest days, still able to be me in my own skin, lots of sports and allowed, tolerated or accepted as a tomboy. I always thought accepted, and that was until I had my one-to-one interview with my form tutor to discuss who I wanted to go to upper school with. I'll never forget the look on her face when she said I think you will have to put down some girls on the form and you can't choose boys. The only problem was I had only ever played playground footie and didn't really know any girls.

That hurdle was jumped and I spent the next five years of schooling, trying to fit in, giving up my love of football, but still playing other 'girls' sports and really closing down my friendship group because it was easier to pretend to just a few people. The AIDS 'Don't Die of

Ignorance' campaign of 1987 had been so hard-hitting and scaremongering it made a young gay woman feel even more alone and isolated.

1991 saw A Level results and university or the chance to move to a city and 'become a lesbian.' By this time I knew what I was, I just didn't know how to be it! Unfortunately, life in Leicester was no easier and lesbian life didn't just happen, so after four terms I decided to drop out and head home to that small village in Bedfordshire. The next two years were spent trying to live a 'straight' life in a small office, wearing a skirt; the elderly owner of the company didn't like girls wearing trousers and answering the phone.

A turning point was on the horizon, and it came to life at the start of the new academic year in 1994. I landed a job in a special school, as a support worker, working with children with complex needs. The school was residential (for students and staff alike) and run by Scope. For the first time ever I learnt about all sorts of people needs, differences and strengths. Three life changing things happened during my two and a half years there: I loved working with children, I was good at it and had a real sense of pride in what I was doing, I fell in love with a woman and I met Paul. The love was unrequited and I was let down so gently, and with such kindness I was even more determined to live as an out woman.

Paul joined the school in September 1996, and we soon became best friends. He had just allowed himself to admit to being gay, and together we trod the road of coming out. Both of us have been very lucky that our families have always been totally accepting and supportive; I really don't know what would have happened had that not been the case.

I left the school and moved north to rural Scotland to manage a group home for adults with learning difficulties; this was an interesting time, a young English lesbian in charge didn't please all of my co-workers. However, the organisation itself was very equal opportunities minded, and it remains the only application form that I have ever filled in which didn't ask for a title, dob, gender or any dates – and this was 1997! By this time I had 'come out' in all aspects of life, although without any real issue I did begin to understand the lifelong commitment to coming out, but living as myself was truly liberating.

I have always wanted to do my very best and have always taken opportunities to develop my skills, earn a promotion and take on extra responsibilities. As such I got to the point in social care where I had reached the end of the line without a qualification. So, in for a penny, in for a pound, I decided to uproot and head home to Bedfordshire to undertake a four-year primary BEd. The desire to teach had always bubbled just under the surface and this was the time to go for it. My application arrived with the University and Colleges Admissions Service the day before the A level results were published in 1998 and through clearing I secured a place at the University of Hertfordshire, I moved home (over 400 miles), worked my notice and said goodbye to Scotland all within five weeks!

My university life this time was great. I loved training to be a teacher, and I had a good group of mature student friends and living off campus was perfect for me. To make ends meet Paul got me a job in the care home he was working in Stevenage and my life fell into a work and study routine for four years. During each of my placements, I was careful not to openly reveal my sexuality and I always spoke about my partner in non-gender specific ways. To be honest most people just need to look at me to know I am gay – I have a strong gaydar rating – but in those days of Section 28 it was wise to keep a low profile. I also knew that returning to university at 25 was my one chance so I couldn't afford for anything to go wrong.

As I approached the final weeks of my final year, I booked an appointment with my personal tutor as hiding myself in school had become somewhat of a chore and I started to feel resentful of it. I had now spent over eight years working for organisations that were fully subscribed to the equal opportunities agenda, and I liked living an authentic life. I asked my tutor about how out can I been in my Newly Qualified Teacher (NQT) year and future career, quickly qualifying that I would never dream of telling the children or parents, and I was merely asking about colleagues and the advice given was 'I wouldn't take that chance – it's just not worth it.' So after all of the freedoms I had enjoyed back in the closet I went (professionally anyway).

My first school was a three-form entry junior school and I was baptised in year 6. My colleagues were wonderful in so many ways and without much of a worry I shared my partner's name and outed myself, funnily enough the world didn't end and I was out amongst the staff; I am sure it was an open secret with the parents and probably the kids too. I spent six very happy years at this school – my first cohort turn 27 this year and I am friends with some on social media. To my knowledge four of the children I taught during that time are now in same-sex relationships, three married – they have all beaten me to that goal in life, and it feels me with immense pride to see their photos and to finally be able to send a message of support and love.

During this time Paul also had the call into teaching and completed his training too. September 2008 saw me take on a Deputy Head Teacher role in a one form entry primary and the following January Paul also joined the staff – in those early days we met at the kettle in the staffroom, he joked 'get out the way deputy dyke' and at this point another colleague nearly dropped her drink and exclaimed, 'you can't call her that, she's our deputy head!' She didn't realise Paul and I had been friends for over a decade, but at least we were out again amongst our colleagues. Paul worked in the behaviour unit and had received a number of homophobic attacks and verbal abuse from one of the students. This was a hugely difficult time for us both. However, a new head arrived and we asked if it were possible that we could come out to the school community; she thought about it and gave it the tentative go ahead.

These things are difficult to plan and sometimes just occur. We found ourselves both accompanying a Year 6 trip to Pizza Express (other pizza trips are available) when one of the girls started being highly opinionated about different families. Paul and I stole a look across the pizzas and both came out with a version of I'm gay and my life is good. The look of shock on her face remains with me today and the domino effect of passing the 'gossip' down the table was visible. For different reasons and nothing to do with sexuality, Paul and I both left that school six months later and went our separate ways.

In a state of emotional turmoil after the sudden passing of my father, I found myself as a Year 5 teacher in a two-form entry junior school, still in the same town as I had always worked. I found myself in back full-time in the classroom and back in the closet – the head had expressly said I don't think our families would like you to be out. Now in 2012 I couldn't believe this was the case. The country was gripped in Olympic fever and I had thought we had turned many corners. However, my two years and a term there were to change my life forever.

Unbeknown to me as soon as I walked into the school one on the teaching assistants (who I was to later work daily with) saw me and knew in her heart that one day we would get married. She kept this secret for over 18 months and strange as it appears when written down by the time that she told me, my feelings for her were quite reciprocated. As you can imagine us, being in a relationship and working in the same school wasn't going to be easy. We took the decision that I would move on and she would stay for another year while she finished her access course and then started on a fulltime BEd herself.

Having been through middle school myself as a child, working in one had always been appealing to me and living on the Herts/Beds border this was a possibility, and in September 2014, I found myself with a Year 6 tutor class teaching in a middle school. A number of things aligned straight away: my partner teacher in my NQT year was the Head of Year 5, a new headteacher started at the same time as I did and bizarrely it was a CofE school. As I didn't know any better, I walked into the head's office early on and had the 'can I be gay?' conversation; she said, "I don't know our community – our children, parents and governors, well – but this is a community school serving all children and supporting all types of family, and this extends to staff too – I will support you as I need to."

Relief flooded through me and I truly felt confident for the first time ever to be my real self. Overheard conversations about someone's trainers being gay were suddenly easy to deal with, 'I am gay, you can call me gay, but those trainers are just not to your taste, they don't fancy other trainers...' and through, sometimes humorous, interactions a wider education began to take place.

With the classes I have always taught, relationships have always been very important. I have always shared my family with my career, my parents and later my mum have always come to see Christmas plays, etc. It was great to be able to talk about what Jo and I had been doing for the weekend, etc., and respond personally to what the children had been doing. When I arrived at the school, there were two other lesbians on the staff: one married 18 months or so after I started and she told her class about the wedding and shared some of the photographs – I am not sure that this would have happened had I not been so open about my own life. The other often says I wish I could be more like you and I certainly wish I had had an open teacher when I was at school. There was just no one in the 1970s (I couldn't agree more).

As Jo (my partner) got into her studies, there were times when she volunteered to do extra things at school, for instance, accompanying us on school trips and completing her research project, and during the long summer holidays from university she worked as a temporary teaching assistant. This was transformational for us both; we were open with the children and staff alike and no one batted an eyelid.

During 2018–2017 a child in one of our feeder schools transitioned to female. Staff at our school were worried about us getting it right when she made the move to our school. I was asked if I was happy to move into Year 5 to be her form tutor and also taken on the role of LGBT+ Champion in our school. I jumped at this chance and quickly ensured my email signature and school badge displayed this title along with my other responsibilities. It was a role I have grown into and develop continually.

It was because of this role that my opening line of a staff presentation included the now famous phrase 'moderately successful lesbian.' I have no idea why I said it, but when I did, 70 plus staff sat up a bit straighter and listened a bit harder. I used my story of how I felt growing up in a world where lesbianism was unheard of and my understanding of what it means to be trans and how we can support our girl who was joining this. Over the years I have delivered many presentations to staff, but this was the first which I received emails of praise and it sparked a real debate, not of different views, but a deep sense of questioning so we could all get it right.

During that school year, I set up!dentity Club, a lunchtime meeting for anyone who felt that their identity was different to others. Some children came out as bi, others as gay, some came because it was safe to be their true ASD self and others because they were the sons and daughters of military families.

Although as a school we haven't promoted my role – i.e. it hasn't gone out full page on the front of the newsletter – it has seeped out naturally and the school community is aware. Early on in 2019 we received an email from some parents requesting a meeting with the form tutor, Deputy Head for pastoral and myself. Two worried parents and a child arrived, and then a deep sigh from one of the parents signalled them to explain how their child wanted to transition and how could we support this. This was a conversation that included much laughter and totally honesty lead to two happy parents, one happy child and three delighted professionals leaving the office that day.

## Epilogue

Paul moved to Cornwall in May 2015. It took a while to secure a permanent job, but he is now working a very small primary school, he is open at work and his husband often attends whole school events.

Jo qualified as a primary teacher in June 2019 and secured an NQT position in my school. She is currently teaching Year 5 while I am based in Year 6 and Year 7. The whole school community know we are a couple and couldn't be more supportive.

I still prioritise my role as LGBT+ champion and with my work with the school council I am planning our first Pride Parade in June.

In the week before half term I was asked to talk to a group of children about saying someone was from 'gaytown' and my favourite interaction was with a burly Year 7 as we passed on the staircase – it went something like this:

| | |
|---|---|
| Y7: | Alright Miss Sharp |
| Me: | Hiya |
| Y7: | Is it true you are going out with Mrs F? |
| ME: | Yep, she's my girlfriend, we've been living together for over 5 years now |
| Y7: | Perfect 'O' Face! |

## Big gay notes from the editor

*Another chapter and another personal account of how young LGBT+ people suffer from deep internal struggles related to their identity. The anecdotal evidence is extensive and the data – where it exists – supports it. Nicola explores how we can use our own experiences to improve those of LGBT+ young people. As I wrote in my opening chapter, I became a teacher for this very reason, but it took me a long time to know quite how I would do it.*

*It can begin with small steps. 'I walked into the head's office early on and had the "can I be gay?" conversation,' says Nicola, and to her relief the response was supportive. Like in Chapter 6, a conversation with the headteacher can be the first step if you are unsure but ultimately their reaction may be the difference between whether you choose to stay at that school or whether you choose to move on to somewhere else.*

*In this chapter, we have a 'moderately successful lesbian,' in Chapter 2 we have a 'legendary lesbian' and LGBTed co-founder and director Hannah Jepson has on many occasions referred to herself as a 'professional lesbian.' Embracing our labels openly is a way to enable great progress. Being authentic = being professional.*

# 21 The rainbow armadillo
*Darrell Chart-Boyles*

*Darrell Chart-Boyles is Deputy Head of Colchester Royal Grammar School. Qualifying in Cardiff, he has 16 years of experience and has taught in four very different schools, from a large Welsh valleys comprehensive to single-sex state and grammar schools. He holds Specialist Leader of Education status for his work supporting equality and diversity at secondary school level, and he achieved a Stonewall School Champion Silver Award for his work on lesbian, gay, bisexual, trans and others (LGBT+) inclusivity at his previous school.*

Looking back, there were so many complex questions behind my decision to stay firmly in the closet: Was I 100% comfortable with my own identity? Would the school support me if I came out? How would my students react – would it affect my classroom management or the respect they had for me? What about their parents? Why weren't there any other openly LGBT+ teachers in the school?

The economically deprived but stunningly beautiful Welsh Valleys was where I began my teaching career in 2004. At 23, I was only a few years older that my sixth form students and the affectionate nickname many of them quickly adopted for me, 'Sir Boy', just highlighted how young I was. The natural curiosity of teenagers, of course, led to lots of them quizzing me about my background, my family, where I lived and my 'girlfriend', and I got used to batting these away with deliberately vague responses.

Geographically, I was distant from the school as a result of a 50-minute drive into the Valleys from where I lived in Cardiff. But I was also socially and emotionally distant from my place of work and my new colleagues. Having been open with colleagues from the first day of my teacher training course, I retreated back into an identity that I'd not really used since before my degree, only talking about my private life with a tiny number of very close colleagues and never within the earshot of students. I was living with my boyfriend of three years, but I barely mentioned him to anyone; he never came to the school and we'd actively avoid my students – and many of my colleagues – if we ever saw them out in Cardiff.

In 2008, while I was still working there, my husband and I had our Civil Partnership ceremony. I'd seen colleagues' weddings celebrated in the staffroom, mentioned in bulletins to parents and congratulated by students, but only my Head of Department and one other close colleague were invited to our wedding, and only a couple of others even knew about it. The fear of revealing too much about myself was probably behind my decision to keep the happiest day of my life so hidden, but that pang regret is there again as I consider the ways in which being my authentic self at such an important moment in my life could have helped the LGBT+ students who were no doubt in each of my classes back then.

When we're discussing LGBT+ experiences over time or preparing for events such as LGBT History Month, I often have to remind my students, and myself, just how much has changed for our community in such a relatively short space of time. My husband and I were civil partnered shortly after it was legalised ('This is Elton John's influence, isn't it?' my mother said when I told her of our engagement), and the Equality Act was still a year away when I joined my second school in 2009.

It wasn't until 2012, when I was working in my third school, that everything really began to change in terms of my visibility as an LGBT+ teacher. The first step was attending one of the unions' LGBT+ teachers' conferences at which I finally met a group of education professionals who were out, honest and open about their sexualities. Extraordinarily, eight years into my teaching career, this was the first time I'd ever spoken to other teachers about anything to do with being LGBT+. Growing up during the era of Section 28 – there it is again – I'd never had any openly gay teachers when I was at school and, whilst I'd suspected I knew the sexuality of several former colleagues, I'd never dared to speak to them about it, preferring instead to keep the kind of cold, hard line between my professional and personal lives that I'd grown so used to.

Energised by my experience at the conference, and now desperate to be just like the teaching professionals I'd spent time with, I returned to school to pitch the Stonewall School Champions programme to my Senior Leadership Team. I was asking for a not inconsiderable sum of money, but I had two aces up my sleeve: I knew Ofsted was increasingly looking at schools' provision in line with the 2010 Equality Act, and I knew that no other school in the local area, with all of whom we were fiercely competitive, had done anything like what I had planned.

Given the green light pretty much instantly, the pathway to that assembly in February 2014 with which I started this chapter was set. We became certified members of the programme; I rewrote the school's Equalities and Behaviour Policies, shared my training with my colleagues, coming out to them en masse as part of the introduction to why it was so important that we were supporting our whole LGBT+ community, and we were then in a position to launch it to our students.

Finding a couple of supportive colleagues with their own personal connections to all things LGBT+, we sketched out our ideas for a student-led LGBT+ Society and planned how we'd pitch it them in a series of assemblies, one to each Key Stage, at the start of LGBT History Month. The assembly took the form of some history of the LGBT+ movement, some background on the Stonewall programme, what we were offering the students in terms of the new society and why we were each getting involved in it.

It was the latter section that would give me the opportunity, for the first time in my career, to be open about my sexuality with my students, but how would I frame it? Some kind of grand coming out wasn't really my style and would detract from one of the key messages I wanted students to take away: your sexuality is only a *part* of what makes you who you are; it doesn't *define* you and being honest about it shouldn't change anyone's perception of you. Sleepless nights led up to that assembly, and I've definitely never been so nervous in front of a hall full of people. In the end, I went with a simple 'as a gay man…' introduction to my section about how I'd never experienced homophobia personally, but how I was determined to eradicate it in our school.

People talk about a 'weight lifting' when you come out as an LGBT+ person and, whilst it's a cliché, it's one grounded in a genuine feeling of relief and a new sense of purpose that lots of LGBT+ people feel once they've taken that step. It was definitely something I felt. In fact, my only regret was not doing it sooner. I was even able to build a popular joke around how gay people never stop 'coming out', but how, delivering this assembly to several hundred people at once, I'd at last managed to make the whole thing a lot more efficient!

The lack of negative reaction was something that I couldn't have dreamt of all those years before when, starting out as a teacher, I carried those hugely damaging fears about being my authentic self in school. Research I've read suggests that being out in the workplace can make people 30% more productive and, while I still felt I was working as flat-out as I always had done, I certainly did so with more of a sense of purpose and motivation than I had done previously; I now had a cause that I was passionate about leading at a whole-school level.

It was a cause that made a tangible impact too. A couple of colleagues came out to me, the LGBT+ Society steadily grew from a handful of LGBT+ students to a large group consisting of them and their allies, LGBT History Month was embedded in the school's calendar of annual events and we successfully applied for Bronze and then Silver Stonewall Awards.

While I worked there, my husband and I decided to become adoptive parents and I couldn't have been better supported. My Head trusted me to update the Parental Leave Policy, I was given all the time off I needed to attend the adoption training and the various approval panels we had to go through, and my colleagues and students bought gifts for our new son, wanted updates and photos while I was off and asked excited, insightful questions about the whole process.

And finally to where I am now: in the words of a colleague, '*very* out' in my role as the Deputy Head of a successful boys' grammar school. For the first time, I mentioned my husband (and our son) in my interview and I introduced myself to my new colleagues, not with some nervy, sweaty-palmed 'coming out' moment but with a matter-of-fact run-down of who I am, my background and my ideologies, that just happened to feature my sexuality.

I discovered during the interview process that the school had an LGBT+ Society already but that it was pretty low-key and that my new Head had already recognised the school was lagging behind with its work in all areas of equalities. Brilliantly, the society had already heard about me before I met them for the first time and, as is tradition for newbies, I was passed the 'rainbow armadillo' to hold while I introduced myself in whatever way I wanted. I went with: 'I'm Mr Chart-Boyles, I'm your new Deputy Head, I'm a married gay man and adoptive parent'. My 2004 teacher self would never have believed it.

Bringing my husband and son to school events, mentioning them occasionally to my students and delivering a new Year 10 Personal Social and Health Education module on 'the right to a family' all mean I've been more open in the last year at my current school than I was at any point during most of my first decade in the profession.

Ultimately then, what's the value of being an open, visible, 'out' Senior Leader? For my students, I'd like to think I can be a role model, someone who's come through some of the things they're struggling with and who's made a success of his career while living an authentic life. I've lost count of the number of young people in this and my previous school who've come out to me and used me as a sounding board for advice on everything from telling their parents, to squaring their faith with their sexuality. For many of them, I was among the first people they'd confided in and it made me think, who would they have told if not me? How long would they have carried round their 'secret' with all its potential negative impacts on their mental health if I hadn't been so obviously someone they could talk to?

I know that I'm still making up for the time I lost in those early years of my teaching career where I was safe in my own little closet, unable to help the LGBT+ students that I had a duty of care for and who would probably have benefitted from me being more visible. But I also know that the rainbow flag on the desk in my office, my high-profile championing of my school's equalities work and finally now being able to be my authentic self are all good for my own mental health as well as, hopefully, making a genuine difference to the lives of some of the brilliant young people with whom I have the privilege to work.

## Big gay notes from the editor

*In this chapter, Darrell once again demonstrates what so many of us have in common. When we become teachers, we often feel the need to 'retreat' back to an identity we adopted before we were 'out'. A performance that can be exhausting. We do this to protect ourselves, and we answer personal questions with intentionally vague responses and self-mediation. I know I barely mentioned any of my relationships at the start of my career, even though heterosexual colleagues' engagements, marriages and babies were celebrated quite openly in staff meetings.*

*Darrell followed a path that worked for him in order that he could finally be his authentic self. He joined an LGBT+ group in his teaching union and met a group of educational professionals who were open and honest about who they were, and he is now a member of our LGBTed network. When he returned to school, he pitched the Stonewall School Champions programme to his leadership team; Continuing Professional Development and a school kite mark are also available through our partnership with the Centre for LGBTQ+ Inclusion in Education at Leeds Beckett University.[1] Finally, he was able to update his school's Equality and Parental Leave policies and eventually be the 'very out' Deputy Head he is today. It may be worth looking at the policies in your own school and see how far they protect you, your colleagues and students. Ofsted is increasingly looking at this in line with the Equality Act 2010.*

*By doing this, we can make a difference to the LGBT+ young people we teach who are indeed, as Darrell says, 'brilliant and a privilege to work with'.*

## Note

1 https://www.leedsbeckett.ac.uk/carnegie-school-of-education/research/centre-for-lgbtq-inclusion-in-education/

# 22 Being the role model I wish I had

*Pam Stallard*

*Pam Stallard is Head of Modern Foreign Languages at Longhill High School in a suburb of Brighton, where she has worked since 2014. A passionate educator who engages with education research and discussion on Twitter, Pam runs a weekly lesbian, gay, bisexual, trans and others (LGBT+) group and the is first point of contact at her school for most students who need support with anything related to gender and sexuality. She loves to travel, even if she doesn't speak the language of the country she's travelling to. She's the one with the pink hair.*

I am a lesbian. I am out to every single member of my school community, by choice.

I first came out as gay when I was 14. I told some friends at school, got my first girlfriend and did a bit of hesitant internet searching about being gay. I didn't know the term LGBT+, and the only gay person I knew in real life was a teacher at my school. I had my suspicions about two others, but this was never confirmed. I have come out almost every day since then to one person or another. It gets easier, but it is still necessary to let people know that I am not straight, and people inevitably have questions.

On my Postgraduate Certificate In Education, we were advised to keep personal details to a minimum, and I took this to mean that mentioning my sexuality on either placement would be taboo. I kept quiet and didn't meet any out LGBT+ teachers or students in this time. I had been out to everyone at university, including leading the Pride society for a year, and so this change was a huge shock to my system. I knew it was legal to discuss LGBT+ content in schools and was confused as to why I wasn't able to be myself at work. However, I didn't want to rock the boat.

The first time I heard *any* mention of homosexuality, bisexuality or trans (an umbrella term used for anyone who is not a cisgender man or woman – meaning that they do not identify with the gender that was assigned to them at birth) in my career which was in my third year of teaching. Unfortunately for me at the time, it was *my* sexuality that was being discussed. I was head of year 10 and maintaining a healthy work–life balance of which I was very proud, when a group of students dug deep through a friend's Facebook and found an old photo of me on a girls' weekend in Manchester's gay village. I was with my then partner and two other gay women, in front of the Canal Street sign. The photo flew around the school like wildfire via social media. The school and I worked together to play it down and to ensure that my reputation was not tarnished. As a lesbian working in a school with over 80% devout Muslim students and parents, I had to assume (although did not know for sure) that I would have had a very difficult time working there if my sexuality was revealed to the community. I was very afraid of what might happen if I were outed to my students and their families. From what I heard from students and spoke about with my colleagues, I was right. For the first time, I felt threatened in my chosen career because of my sexuality, and this felt extremely intimidating. I felt self-conscious and concerned of the possible repercussions, both personal and professional. Thankfully, I was supported by the senior leadership team, and the furore over the photos soon died down once the students saw that neither I nor senior management was taking the bait. The students moved on to the next big thing. There was minimal sanction for the students involved, despite what I saw as a gross invasion of my privacy and right to a personal life. It's worth mentioning that through this whole experience, my social media was absolutely locked down to private, and these photos were untagged and posted by a friend. I completed my year as their head of year and went back to full-time French teaching at the start of the following academic year.

I met one Year 11 student who was not quiet about his sexuality, but I didn't dare come out even to him. He was the root of the single homophobic incident I escalated whilst I worked there. Another student made a joke about dropping the soap, and I knew that I had to defend him. The perpetrator was sanctioned, but there was no reparative education for him. I felt awful for the student and couldn't imagine how he must feel, but I was not confident enough to out myself in support of him.

In my final term, I was asked to deliver training to staff on managing homophobic language in the corridors and classrooms following a spate of comments such as 'that's so gay' being heard around the school. I duly obeyed but unfortunately didn't see any staff using my tips or advice.

I always desperately wanted to be out, working there, and my life was changing fast. A few months after the Canal Street incident, I got engaged. I told my colleagues to whom I was out, and everyone was over the moon for me. However, I took my ring off to teach my classes because I didn't want to lie to my students, and avoiding the conversation was the only way to do that. Prior to this, I hadn't been ashamed of my sexuality for any reason in nearly five years. After I got married, there was no way I could let fear shame me into keeping the ring off any longer. I was leaving in July, just a few short months away. Safe in the knowledge that I was moving to a job in leafy-green Brighton – the well-known LGBT+ capital of the United Kingdom, I put my ring on and refused to lie any further. Surprisingly few questions were asked. I suspected that my students may have guessed over the years or heard on the grapevine after the photo went around the school like a virus. I remember one year 7 girl who stayed back after class to discuss how to say particular words from her faith in French. She complimented my ring and asked about my husband. When I explained that I had just married a woman, she didn't skip a beat. She asked about what we both wore – if we both wore dresses, if there was a sharp suit – even though this was years ahead of Cara Delevigne normalising the gender-bending of a woman attending a wedding in a tux. Teeth gritted, I pulled out my phone and showed her a couple of my wedding photos. She said they were beautiful. When I got home, I cried. I felt so torn between my desire to be myself and let the students see the normality of LGBT+ people and my fear of prejudice or judgement.

Brighton beckoned, and I followed the call. If anyone asked, I was honest. Married, to a woman, just a few months, really happy. Not even a sniff of a problem. It was all *fine*. I loved it; it was a huge relief to not have to hide, and I felt so much better. I gleefully joined the staff LGBT+ group, and we supported students who came out through the use of one-to-one mentoring and the help of a local group called Allsorts,[1] with whom we still work now. They visit Longhill High to talk to students face to face, giving support with all kinds of issues surrounding LGBT+ life, and meet with parents and significant family members where necessary. Allsorts have been particularly fantastic with several trans students who have come out over their years at Longhill. We organised an annual LGBT+ day for Year 7 students, also through Allsorts. A bundle of rainbow lanyards were dutifully purchased and distributed. It's wonderful for staff and students to be able to identify allies on the faculty through something as simple as a publicly worn rainbow lanyard, and I would recommend this to all schools that want to support their LGBT+ students and staff.

However, this was the extent of our work. I heard reports that some staff were uncomfortable delivering the sex education portion of Personal, Social and Health Education (PSHE) and therefore LGBT+ themes often dropped by the wayside too. The separate topic of LGBT+ history wasn't taught until Year 11, where in the days of social media and the internet, was often years after students had started coming to terms with their sexuality. And there are more and more of these individuals every year.

There was a group for students held half-termly where they could meet and socialise. This was reasonably well attended, but I estimated from my conversations with the students that more than half the room were there in support of a friend, rather than there as LGBT+ as a number in our school. I was overwhelmed by the support of these allies, as I am often still now by allied behaviour in my family and friends.

However, even schools in the most accepting of areas will have their own problems. I recognised a lot of anti-LGBT+ languages around schools and knew that in an era where Stonewall 'That's So Gay' posters were rife around the city, they needed to be rife around the schools too. A knowledge and acceptance of the gay community is not innate, and it needs to be educated. After a particular incident in July 2018, a colleague approached me and said he wanted to take action on casual homophobia and use of offensive language. I agreed that something could be done, and he showed me a video of a teacher – Daniel Tomlinson-Gray, now co-founder and director of *LGBTed* – coming out in assembly in support of students. He suggested that we speak to the year group we were most concerned about and, in doing so, out ourselves in support of the message we were giving. We hoped that by saying, 'it's not banter, we're gay and we're offended by what you're saying', we would put these students in a situation where they had no further excuse except hatred to use the language, and we desired the complete elimination of words or phrases like 'don't be gay' or 'you're so gay', 'fag', 'queer', 'homo' and 'dyke'. In a social environment filled with hormones and pressure from all sides, we were demanding their focus and, for some, a dramatic change in their behaviour. However, we were also laying ourselves absolutely open. We had full senior leadership team (SLT) support for these assemblies, but we were the ones who would be on the receiving end of any backlash at all. And homophobia hurts.

We delivered the assembly in July 2018. Our community had just commemorated the second anniversary of the Pulse attacks in Orlando, and the city was warming up for Brighton Pride. I had a nearly two-year-old son, and a freshly broken-down marriage. I was ready for a fight if I had to be. Happily, my adrenaline was flowing for nothing – the assembly was a knock-out. It ended with applause, and a student came up to my colleague shortly after and thanked him. SLT asked us to repeat it for the four other year groups, and this was accepted in a heartbeat. It was clear to anyone who knew our school and our students that this would be a success in reducing reports of homo-, bi- and trans-phobia, but that it would also ensure that students would be more likely to report if there *were* an issue.

I am proud to say that our actions have led to a dramatic reduction in incidents of homo-, bi- and transphobic language and bullying at school, and these are now dealt with in a whole different manner. Following the first occurrence, a student has an education session with a member of staff, often myself. This is to ensure they are fully aware of their actions and the consequences if they choose to continue that behaviour. We also contact home to inform that the harmful behaviour has occurred. A second offence will result in a sanction, as we know by this stage that the student is choosing to behave that way. I find it so important that our students are educated and given a chance to change.

Outing myself as a gay teacher has led students to feel safe and confident in approaching me with LGBT+ issues. The most challenging cases that I deal with tend to be those which they initiate via email – it's a safe way for students to contact me whilst not identifying their need to do so to friends. My tactic when this happens is firstly to get a response to the student as soon as possible, so that they know they are not alone and that someone is listening. This is especially important over a weekend or summer holiday, when our students can be more at risk due to isolation from their normal means of emotional support. I consider safeguarding and report when I know it is necessary, prioritising protecting a student who may be at risk from someone else or from themselves. I then arrange to meet discreetly with the student (with another adult present if necessary), and my first question is always 'What do you want to happen?' Sometimes this leads to outside support from external organsiations, but more often me personally spending time with that young person and allowing them to talk through what's going on for them. My free time as a head of department and full-time teacher is limited, so I also signpost them to relevant online or in-person services, which in Brighton we are very lucky to have. I suggest they attempt to attend our LGBT+ group for support and identify allies in the school environment. Whilst we have a high proportion of staff who are LGBT+ and a huge number of allies (naturally), this is not always evident to students and can be hugely supportive for them at a time where they need solidarity and a team around them.

There have, of course, been times where I have had to admit 'I can't help in this situation' or 'I can't help right now', and both myself and the students have had to get our heads around this. One student was part of a particular religious group where coming out would mean complete separation from their family, and the discussion we had was that it just wasn't possible for them at that time, at their age. We have maintained contact, and this student is doing well, despite the possible difficulties this could have caused. For others, it has been about saying, 'I think you just need to wait a while' or 'Perhaps this needs to be introduced more slowly and with more care'. Situations like this are harrowing – the kind that sends me home thinking about them, frantically googling for case studies where a similar situation has had a happy ending. Working with the LGBT+ students at school has really shown me that my power is limited, and sometimes a case has to be left to time and the willpower of the student involved. I have also had to learn patience through waiting for referrals from social services and requesting support from external agencies, which are often pushed for funding and time. This has really motivated me to be a better leader for them in several ways. Firstly, I have had to create a support network for myself – friends and allies on the school staff to whom I know I can talk when things are difficult for me, researchers and other LGBT+

teachers on Twitter with whom I can discuss challenging situations and, more frequently than I had expected, the students themselves.

We now have a weekly student group attended by around 25 pupils. Our members are LGBT+ students, allies and their friends. The sessions are generally student led – often I will have short one-to-one discussions and catch up with the students, and we welcome any new members. If there's been LGBT+ events in the news, we watch clips and discuss these, and obviously there's a lot of mention of popular culture, both LGBT+ related and otherwise. I actively encourage staff to come along to the group – this is because I need the students to be aware that the teachers they see every day are their allies, their supporters, that we all have their backs.

I'd really like to tell a particular story about a student who has affected me, or brought me to the edge of tears, or inspired me, but I honestly know that those would not be my stories to tell. We may have made colossal progress in recent years, but there is huge ground yet to cover, especially for trans members of the community. The students in my group have faced bullying at school and at home, and many struggle with self-harm and with anxiety, depression or other mental health conditions. Some have stressful difficulties with behaviour or their home life, conflicts with personal opinions, older siblings or religion, and lots are still working on coming out of the closet. But they are all an absolute inspiration to me.

## Big gay notes from the editor

*In this chapter, Pam is another example of a teacher who was told in her early years to 'keep personal details to a minimum'. This is a vague and usually loaded sentiment offered mainly to LGBT+ teachers. Like in Chapter 21, Pam had to retreat back into a former identity once she left university because she 'didn't want to rock the boat' as a new teacher. This fear of 'rocking the boat' is dominant in the psyche of many a trainee LGBT+ teacher; many of us are taught to fit in with our school and keep our heads down. I learned very quickly the hard way how important it is in some schools to not have ideas 'above your station' – to some, this includes talking about LGBT+ equality and expressing your own identity – and I eventually had to decide what was important to me.*

*'Brighton beckoned and I followed the call', writes Pam. I made the same journey to Brighton for university and was instantly seduced by how eccentric, tolerant and liberal it is. I try not to take this for granted, but it is clear that some schools in the local area make the mistake of assuming that there is no work to be done in ensuring LGBT+ children feel safe and included. I have heard on more than one occasion in local schools that 'it's not a problem around here'. However, all schools are required to record specific incidents of homophobic, transphobic and biphobic bullying and show how they have been dealt with.*

*Our duty as teachers is to our students. Being a visible LGBT+ role model ensures that LGBT+ students know they are not alone and that someone is listening. Over a weekend or during a Summer holiday, in particular, students may feel more isolated or not able to access the support they need. We can be there for them by email, which is a safe way for them to make contact without 'outing' themselves to friends, or we can direct them to local support services. We cannot be complacent; we must ensure all LGBT+ students and staff are welcome in our schools and we must mean it when we say it.*

## Note

1 https://www.allsortsyouth.org.uk/parents-carers

# 23 Changing the narrative
Why being 'out' at school is so important

*Will Goldsmith*

*Will Goldsmith is Director of Teaching and Learning at Latymer Upper School in Hammersmith, West London. He is a progressive at heart, working with lesbian, gay, bisexual, trans and others (LGBT+) students in his school, championing equality and diversity at managerial level. When not teaching the nation's youth, he also sings with the Fourth Choir, an LGBT+ choir who perform lots of fabulous gigs in London and beyond.*

I first came across the idea of coming out to my students when I was training to be a teacher in an inner London school in 2005. The charity Stonewall had put out a video where a teacher was talking about being openly gay to his classes, espousing the idea of role-modelling. I remember thinking that, despite being openly gay to family, friends and even colleagues, the idea of sharing such information with my students was genuinely terrifying. I would regularly have nightmares where I'd be in a lesson and a child would ask me, 'Are you gay sir?' and I wouldn't know how to deal with it. Even when I was awake, I couldn't formulate anything I felt comfortable with as a result – all those memories of being bullied at school about being gay came flooding back, and they were always situations where, whatever I said, the boys in my single-sex school would twist my words so I was humiliated, whether I denied it or evenly vaguely acknowledged it as a possibility.

Looking back on my career so far (it's now nearly 14 years I've been in the profession), I now understand that my own experience of being a gay boy in school has shaped so much of who I am in a professional context, just as, on a wider level, so much of how teachers behave in their work is influenced by their own educational experiences. While I did eventually come out at the age of 17 to my schoolmates, I think I would have been ready to come out around the age of 12 or 13 if I'd been in a more benign environment. Tellingly, that delay in being able to be more honest about myself within my community has been mirrored in my career as a teacher as it was only in 2016, when I started at my current school in leafy, liberal West London, that I felt able to share my sexuality with my students from the start. Even then, it wasn't easy, not so much because of the school but because of my own instinct for self-censorship. Luckily, my school already had a student LGBT+ society where students would meet fortnightly to discuss issues relating to sexuality and gender, and it so happened that it needed a new teacher to run it as the previous member of staff had just left the term before. No one else amongst my colleagues seemed inclined to run it, but I felt strongly enough about such a precious group that it must be run so, despite some trepidation, I committed to running it myself.

That bold step was over four years ago now and, looking back on that time, I have come a long way. While the society has had its ups and downs under my stewardship, and there are times when I really don't feel like I'm doing a very good job, I am certain that I'm in a much better position personally and professionally. I also feel like it's vital for me to keep up the work I do, not only with the students but also with other colleagues, parents and the wider community. There are days when it can feel exhausting bringing up LGBT+ issues in my lessons, meetings and conversations – sometimes I have nagging thoughts that I'm making too much of a fuss or there are more important things to campaign for or I'm simply being self-indulgent – but what stops me from giving up are the people around me who are still suffering as a result of homophobia and transphobia, the daily examples of heteronormativity and well-meaning but misinformed approaches to students and staff who are LGBT+.

One challenge in writing this is the thought of people thinking that I am being overly critical of my current school – far from it! I've never worked in such an inclusive and welcoming school for LGBT+ staff, students and parents. Certainly, by the time our students reach the Sixth Form, they very rarely have to deal with homophobia from their peers, and, as a teacher, I am comfortable wearing my Pride badge around the school and talking about my (male) partner to my students when it happens to come up – something made easier by the fact that he's also an English teacher! I am always aware of how lucky I am to be living and working in a time when schools are legally permitted to educate their students about LGBT+ sexuality without fear of censure, when the laws of the land are, in the main, just to the LGBT+ community. However, as with society as a whole, there are still things that could be improved (as they could in other aspects of what we do as a school – improvement is a never-ending story in education!) and unless people like me speak up, students and staff in schools will, as a result of their sexuality and gender identities, continue to suffer needlessly. The statistics are unambiguous in terms of the disproportionately damaged mental health of LGBT+ pupils at school, and the legacy of this suffering lasts a lifetime. In the future, some of those young people will go on to be teachers themselves and our education system and therefore society will be better off if they have better mental health than my generation.

Measuring impact is always very difficult in terms of culture and social environments; however, there are a few instances in the past three years of running an LGBT+ student group and being an openly gay teacher where I can testify to at least some small-scale positive impact. The first moment is the most recent – as part of my role as Assistant Headteacher, I am in charge of new staff induction and, amongst the new teachers who started in September, is a Newly Qualified Teacher who asked if our school has rainbow lanyards available for staff. Whatever the merits or not of wearing such lanyards, the more profound affirmation I had about his request is that it started off an ongoing conversation about visibility, role-modelling and institutional improvement. We currently do not have an equality and diversity committee in the school, even though such concerns are part of much of what we do, but we are now exploring the idea of setting one up as a result of his suggestion. While it's early days on this front, the fact that he could see a senior leader 'flying the flag' gave him the confidence not only to come out to his students (he wears his rainbow lanyard every day to work) but also to challenge us as an institution to improve, not just how we work on LGBT+ inclusion but equalities more generally.

The second specific thing is also on a small scale but has been perhaps the most emotionally charged – working with parents of LGBT+ students. While it's not always been straightforward – some parents of the students I work with have struggled with the changing gender identity of their children, for example, or they worry that coming out in your early teens can lead to stigmatisation – I also have seen genuine gratitude from some parents that their children have a teacher who they trust and can talk to about their sexuality. One parent recently requested a meeting with me, not to talk about her own child but to see if we could lay on talks for all parents about LGBT+ issues facing teenagers because she wanted them to benefit from the individual support she'd received from me. Seeing other people, especially LGBT+ 'allies' calling for us to do more as a school really helps motivate me to continue what I do and banish those doubts that beset me at times.

As for the students themselves, I'm not sure the extent to which they feel I am a role model as such – which self-respecting teenager wants to be a teacher for goodness sake?! However, I am proud of the work I have done, however inexpertly, in facilitating and encouraging them in what they do to express their queerness in an environment that often, by its nature, frowns on nonconformity. We have run LGBT History Month assemblies for the last two years, marched in London Pride as part of the main parade, advised the Head of PSHE on including LGBT+ specific content for the sex ed modules and hosted numerous talks on topics ranging from the politics of camp to queer film, and we are now seeing students from the younger years start to take a greater role in the society.

Finally, thinking about myself, knowing that I can be free to talk about having a male partner in lessons without having to neutralise his gender when I'm teaching and the thought just comes into my head – being an English teacher means that relationships pop up all the time, that I can be free to be camp without feeling shame and that I can run a school trip to London Pride without even blinking; all of these things and more have banished those nightmares about being asked 'are you gay, sir?' completely. Being free of that shame and fear undoubtedly makes me happier in myself and professionally. However, I also know that what I get to experience in my school, even with the improvements that are yet to be made, is a very rare and precious thing. When I worked outside of London in the Home Counties, I never really thought I could or should be openly gay to my students – it felt dangerous or bordering on the inappropriate. The argument in my head would always be that, if I were a heterosexual male teacher, I wouldn't walk into a classroom and tell my students I had sex with women. I also came across several teachers who were still in the closet, something which they often linked to fears about what would happen if the parents and students at school found out. While there are high-profile cases in the media of parents protesting outside schools in Birmingham, what disturbs me more is the thought of countless teachers who cannot be themselves in their place of work. Who you love and what your gender identity is forms a fundamental part of your identity, even if it is not all of who you are. If teachers are not able to be themselves, then their students will undoubtedly suffer, whatever their sexuality or gender. If their teachers are not out and proud, how will they become so? How will they grow up to be adults who embrace diversity?

Being an English teacher, I have read a lot of LGBT+ literature and I am often depressed by the way so many of them are bleak narratives which so often end in heartache, pain and even death. Even E. M. Forster's *Maurice*, a gay love story which does not end tragically, was only published posthumously; such was Forster's fear of persecution during his life time. While things have changed a lot since 1970, there are still so many stories – fictional and real – that end unhappily for LGBT+ people in our world. My tale (fingers crossed) is one that has, professionally *and* personally, followed a much more positive plotline than the norm, and I hope, in sharing it, I can play a small part in changing the societal 'narrative' about LGBT+ teachers for the better.

## Big gay notes from the editor

*In our penultimate chapter, experienced school leader Will Goldsmith writes about the small steps we can all take to change the narrative in schools about LGBT+ teachers. His first specific example is making rainbow lanyards available for staff. Though this may appear to be 'tokenism', it is effective and it can work as part of an ongoing process to 'usualise' LGBT+ visibility. As Will says, it can lead to honest conversations about other ways in which the school can improve. As teachers and leaders, we should ask ourselves how comfortable we are having those conversations.*

*Secondly, parental talks are a great way to engage parents with LGBT+ issues facing teenagers. As I have said previously, it can be exhausting as the 'out teacher' who has to do all the ground work – and arguably it is not the LGBT+ teachers with the training needs in this area – so our allies in the school community are incredibly important. Having allies – whether amongst parents or staff – can motivate us to continue with the work we are doing.*

*Furthermore, Will suggests encouraging young people to express their 'queerness' is another way to support them. We have heard in previous chapters, directly from former students, about how Drama and English lessons in particular have helped shaped young LGBT+ students' identities by encouraging nonconformity. Where does 'queerness' exist in your curriculum and how can you adapt your schemes of work to actualise queerness? The author of Chapter 3, David Lowbridge-Ellis, has also written about 'Queering the Curriculum' for our partners at the Centre for LGBTQ+ Inclusion in Schools.[1] It is full of practical ideas about how to make the curriculum more LGBT+ inclusive in all subjects in your school.*

*Finally, we must be visible and authentic LGBT+ teachers because our students need us to be. As Will suggests, 'if their teachers are not out and proud, how will students become so? How will they grow up to be adults who embrace diversity?'*

*Let's be the role models we needed when we were at school.*

## Note

1 'This knowledge organiser is queer. It's here. Get using it', https://leedsbeckett.ac.uk/-/media/files/research/lgbtq-june-final.pdf?la=en

# 24 Being your authentic self at work

*Hannah Jepson*

*Hannah Jepson is co-founder and director of LGBTed. A qualified business psychologist, Hannah successfully led and managed a range of large-scale selection, talent management and Diversity and Inclusion strategy projects nationally. She is a member of the National Equality and Diversity Forum for education and works with the Department for Education to develop the national lesbian, gay, bisexual, trans and others (LGBT+) education strategy. She is a published academic author whose work on the career experiences of gay women in the UK has been featured in an international research handbook exploring diversity and careers. In this final chapter, Hannah concludes with what we at LGBTed mean by being authentic at work.*

> Pretending is hard, pretending takes time and effort and energy you simply don't have when you are revising for your exams, or applying for jobs, or trying to do your job.
>
> Anon LGBT+ teacher

I want to tell you a story. When I was in the first few years of my career I moved down to Southampton – for a relationship. With a woman. Let's just be clear about that now as the rest of the story may feel a little odd. I got a job and I was working in HR. It was a great job with good prospects. I had experienced no overt homophobia and that wasn't the driver for the events that followed.

During the first few weeks of getting to know each other, we were sharing stories about ourselves and our lives – the girls I worked with seemed lovely, funny, kind, honest and I had no reason to believe they would react badly. But I lied. I lied through my teeth. I made up a boyfriend, Tom. Tom didn't take on the characteristics, family, career or any elements of my actual girlfriend's life – I made the whole thing up, as if I was drafting a character backstory for a Hollywood film. I spent hours in the evening inventing little quirks and stories about Tom.

Looking back I think I did this because I wanted to keep my real life completely out of the picture, because using my girlfriend's details and changing the name was too much of a risk – a risk that in sharing my weekend anecdotes I'd slip up and say she instead of he, and then I'd be found out to be a liar but worse they would know I was gay and that would most certainly not go in my favour. This is what happened in my head – looking back it's such an extreme conclusion to draw without any evidence. Like I said it wasn't the fact that I'd heard any homophobia, but it was the stifling heteronormativity that was palpable to me as soon as stepped foot into the main reception that fuelled my reticence to come out. This isn't an unusual story – I've heard my own story played back to me too many times than I care to remember.

You see the thing is – people assume we're straight, until we share with them some information that tells them otherwise, and in schools this is made more difficult due to the uniquely complex ecosystem of stakeholders that all exists within that environment: young people, professional peers, parents, governors/trustees, non-teaching staff. It isn't as simple as say the message once, one way, let it land and move on. We have to carefully calculate the message, tweak and adapt it, rehearse it and share iterations of it numerous times.

Research by Thoroughgood et al. (2017)[1] explored the notion of paranoid cognition and explained the relation between transgender employees' perceptions of discrimination at work and their job attitudes and well-being. The research defines paranoid cognition as 'hypervigilance, rumination, and sinister attributional tendencies.' The research found that paranoid cognition does affect trans employees' well-being, turnover intentions and emotional exhaustion and how the absence of paranoid cognition makes people more likely to experience job satisfaction and more likely to actually want to stay in their jobs and show commitment to their organisation.

My experience completely aligns with the research – I was on edge all of the time and I couldn't regale you with a story about an actual piece of work I did during my time there because I was so pre-occupied with the lies I needed to tell to keep up with my heterosexual colleagues. I wasn't as good as my colleagues at my job in that time – I should have been absolutely in my prime, just out of university, ready to work and soak it all in but I wasn't and I had one of the worst times of my life in that job. And actually, when I unpicked it, it was simply because I couldn't be myself – imagine spending five days a week, 37.5 hours (it's often more let's be honest) NOT being myself. Not being authentic.

In 2017 I published some research exploring the experiences of gay women in the workplace (Fielden and Jepson 2016).[2] The majority of women I spoke to expressed a strong reluctance to come out at work, not because they experienced the culture of their organisations as overtly homophobic but because of the way that they saw sexism and homophobia cut across each other within their work environments. Those women chose to hide a part of themselves because they couldn't hide the fact that they were women and so they lied, pretended and covered up throughout for almost all of their careers.

I'll say it again. Pretending is hard. Pretending takes time and energy and effort you don't have when you are applying for a job or trying to do your job to the best of your ability and that's when the spiral of stereotyping continues. Because people in minority groups can often experience a very real stereotype threat, and as a result, they have less energy to expend on performing to the best of their abilities at work. The subsequent perception that they are not performing at their best can often be tied up with their identity, and it is from that position that unhelpful and damaging stereotypes are created and perpetuated.

So what does authenticity mean? Well, we can probably agree that it means different things, to different people, and it is totally dependent on our own contexts at the time, right?

Our definition of authenticity is this:

> The feeling of complete and uncontested alignment between yourself, your environment and the people within it allowing you to focus not on compromising yourself and perform any given task as your very best self.

At LGBTed we think it's vitally important that children and staff have authentic role models from the LGBT+ community. The old adage "you can't be what you can't see" rings so true still, and for someone who didn't have any role models at school and went on to hide who I was, I know how damaging that can be. We know self-harm is disproportionately high amongst members of the LGBT+ community, and we know that the average life expectancy of someone from the transgender community is 35. This makes me unbelievably sad that someone should feel so isolated and ashamed to the extent they would harm themselves, often with devastating consequences. If people have authentic role models who are proud to be members of the LGBT+ community that can send such a powerful message to our aspiring leaders of the future (staff and children). It says, "I'm me, and you can be you too."

I wasn't always out at work, but after the experience with 'Tom', I vowed never to hide who I was again. I would be me and I would make sure that I chose places to work that allowed me to do so. I consider myself an authentic role model at work to the teams I work with, and my peers and I am committed to living by these rules every single day.

**L**ead with pride: Talk about what you did at the weekend, be open about who you are, talk about the things that you are passionate about and champion initiatives you feel can make a change. It's important to be a leader who knows who they are and isn't afraid to show it.

**E**nable others to be themselves: By leading with pride, you'll give others the confidence to be themselves. Remember diversity isn't just about LGBT, but it's about diversity of thought, of working style and communication. We need to encourage people not to fit in with the dominant leadership style and to bring their true selves to work.

**S**peak up against homophobia, biphobia and transphobia: For that matter, speak up if hetero and cisnormativity dominate your organisation. People probably don't know they are doing it – but it can be stifling.

**B**e honest: Always. There's a level of professionalism we all need to maintain, but being honest about who you are if you are LGBT isn't about waving a flag and shouting from the rooftops, it's about being comfortable just as your heterosexual colleagues are, to share the mundanities of your life with the people with whom you spend you week with. It doesn't and shouldn't detract from you as a professional person.

**I**ntegrity matters: Even if it feels uncomfortable, it's important to persist in championing diversity and inclusion even if it isn't always easy to do so.

**A**llies are important: As an LGBT role model, it's important to understand who your allies are; they can be a powerful driver of change in your organisation.

**N**ever give up: Never. Give. Up.

Why not write your own?

I am often asked: why do we need diversity, inclusion and authenticity in schools and organisations? My answer: That's like asking why do we need the heating on in the building in winter? It's critically important to our well-being that we see the richness that exists in society and to know that we can be a part of it.

## Notes

1 Thoroughgood, C. N., Sawyer, K. B., & Webster, J. R. (2017) What Lies Beneath: How Paranoid Cognition Explains the Relations Between Transgender Employees' Perceptions of Discrimination at Work and Their Job Attitudes and Wellbeing. *Journal of Vocational Behavior, 103* (Part A), 99–112. https://doi.org/10.1016/j.jvb.2017.07.009.
2 Fielden, S.L. & Jepson, H. (2016) An Exploration into the Career Experiences of Lesbians in the UK. *Gender in Management, 31*(4), 281–296. https://doi.org/10.1108/GM-03-2016-0037.

For Product Safety Concerns and Information please contact our EU
representative GPSR@taylorandfrancis.com
Taylor & Francis Verlag GmbH, Kaufingerstraße 24, 80331 München, Germany

www.ingramcontent.com/pod-product-compliance
Lightning Source LLC
Chambersburg PA
CBHW082050230426
43670CB00016B/2847